The
Caterer and Hotelkeeper
Guide to

Money Matters
for
Hospitality Managers

About the author

Cathy Burgess (MPhil, CdipAF, FBHA, FHCIMA) spent many years in operational and financial management positions in the hospitality industry, principally with Thistle Hotels and Marriott Corporation. She is now a senior lecturer in accounting in the School of Hotel and Restaurant Management at Oxford Brookes University.

She teaches financial management to undergraduate and postgraduate students both in the University and via on-line and distance learning. Cathy has been on the Council of BAHA (British Association of Hospitality Accountants) for many years and is currently their Membership Officer.

In her spare time she plays with her children, gardens with her husband, and helps restore their very old house in the Cotswolds.

The
Caterer and Hotelkeeper Guide to

Money Matters
for
Hospitality Managers

Cathy Burgess

BUTTERWORTH
HEINEMANN

OXFORD AUCKLAND BOSTON JOHANNESBURG MELBOURNE NEW DELHI

Butterworth-Heinemann
Linacre House, Jordan Hill, Oxford OX2 8DP
225 Wildwood Avenue, Woburn, MA 01801-2041
A division of Reed Educational and Professional Publishing Ltd

℞ A member of the Reed Elsevier plc group

First published 2001

TRADEMARKS/REGISTERED TRADEMARKS
Computer hardware and software brand names mentioned in this book are
protected by their respective trademarks and are acknowledged.

British Library Cataloguing in Publication Data
A catalogue record for this book is available from the British Library

ISBN 0 7506 5250 0

For information on all Butterworth-Heinemann publications visit our
website at **www.bh.com**

 Designed and typeset by Elle and P.K. McBride, Southampton

Printed and bound in Great Britain

Contents

Contents

Foreword

Hospitality is generally viewed as a people business. It is a sociable environment with the emphasis on customer care. So why should hospitality managers bother themselves with issues that focus on money and accounts?

Put simply, they need to do so because money matters. In an increasingly competitive market businesses that are finance savvy are likely to be leaner, better run and have the edge over those that are not. At the front door in full view of everyone good hospitality managers are generally adept in caring for their customers. But behind the scenes at the back door they need to be just as focused on improving revenue, reducing costs, and caring for assets.

Looking after money is not just the responsibility of those who are trained accountants. It does not have to be a complicated business; the perception is often worse than the reality. Those who make the effort to look after the pennies are also likely to set a good example to their colleagues. By leading from the top and making it clear that drains on the business such as wastage and theft are unacceptable, managers have the ability to make a huge impact on the bottom line. Small savings mount up and can soon turn into big ones, a move that is likely to be noted (and maybe even rewarded) by those at higher levels.

That's one formula that's not too hard to add up.

Jenny Webster
Deputy Editor
Caterer & Hotelkeeper

Preface

What's the point of this book?

Well, Money Matters! – whether you're working in a mega-corporation operating in 50 countries or helping on a take-away stall – if you don't manage effectively then you'll lose money. You may think that you as an individual aren't important, but you are. Your actions as a manager or supervisor determine how your staff will behave. A pound saved (or made in revenue) on one transaction multiplies to a vast sum when you consider the number of transactions in a day, and so on. Twenty pounds a day is £7,300 a year – enough to pay your wages for several months.

The hospitality industry is enormous, employing around 6% of the UK workforce in its many different sections, all of which have their own individual characteristics. The skills you acquire in one sector can be used in another so although you may think, for instance, that hotels are 'different', many of the features are similar. This is particularly true of the finance area as all key activities are transferable and have an impact on the money aspect in one way or another, across all sectors.

Also, many financial aspects of the hospitality business are common to all industries. For the successful management of any type of business (including those that are non-profit-making) you need to address three main areas:

▷ Improving revenue
▷ Reducing costs
▷ Caring for assets.

Purpose

The purpose of this book is to give you an understanding of how your actions can affect the management of the business and the financial results of these actions. We will look at the different features of the various sectors, and identify many of the areas in which you can help improve efficiency and hence the financial results. You will develop an understanding of the basic principles of financial control and how it can affect the organization as a whole.

You do need 'accounts' to help you do this. However, this *isn't* an accounting book so if you've tried to study 'accounts' before then please don't worry! We will be looking at some of the accounting statements but the approach throughout is to look at management first and then numbers second.

Yes, you CAN do numbers! As long as you can use a (simple) calculator then you will be able to do some of the simple examples that are given in the different chapters. You don't need to be good at number-crunching to be an effective manager, just able to calculate simple exercises. What is important is that you are able to understand the effect of your actions and those of others on the finances of the organization. It's not a textbook either – more of a manual that you'll be able to use both now and in the future.

By the end of this book, therefore, you should be able to:

▷   Understand why the 'bottom-line' is important

▷   Use some of the main techniques to control your area of business

▷   Calculate the effect of your actions in a range of areas.

Structure

This book is divided into 11 chapters. The first two look at the importance of control, the basic accounting statements and how the statements are put together. Chapters 3 and 4 focus on the management of revenue and costs. Chapter 5 looks at pricing issues and Chapter 6 deals with forecasting future levels of business, which is crucial to planning your activities.

Managing cash and stocks appear next – two of the most susceptible areas for losses – and this leads in to standard costing which is a technique essential to sectors with exact recipe specifications, such as airline catering. Chapter 9 looks at spreadsheet skills to help you perform all these tasks more easily. Chapter 10 then looks outside the unit and gives you an insight into how your unit relates to the 'bigger picture' of the whole organization, and why different types of company structure might be relevant to you. The final chapter summarizes the book, gives a brief introduction to forecasting future trends and then considers how you can develop your skills further.

Approach

The approach is very pragmatic and 'hands-on'. You will see lots of real-life examples from a variety of industry sectors (with details changed to protect the innocent- and guilty!) and each section will have some mini-exercises to practice (with answers) so that you know how to use the different techniques.

We assume that you are working, even if only a few hours a week, so you'll also have chance to go and find out how things are practised in your workplace and what makes your business function effectively. If you aren't in employment then use a facility you know – your local pub or café will do fine. Also included are some useful tips. The key word throughout is *control*.

At the end of the book is a reading list of books where you can look if you want to find out more about different areas. Some of these are financially-based, others focus on other disciplines or specific sectors. You will also see a list of web-sites – and you may have others yourself.

Don't forget too that industry journals can be really helpful (e.g. *Caterer and Hotelkeeper* and *Hospitality*) in giving you up-to-date industry practice and ideas about what is happening elsewhere in your own and other sectors.

Acknowledgements

With thanks to Allen, Timothy, Victoria and Rachel for all their patience and advice, and thanks to everyone from 'the industry' who gave their assistance.

1

Introduction to hospitality control

▼
▼
▼
▼
▼

Hospitality and tourism ◄

Features of the industry ◄

Theft ◄

Stakeholders ◄

Organization ◄

Accounts ◄

Introduction

In this chapter we will introduce the concept of 'control' and hospitality in general. We'll also look at the function of the financial control office where some of the control processes take place. As you'll see as we work through further chapters, much of control happens in the operating departments – so control is a business-wide function, not just an accounting one.

By the end of this chapter you should be able to:

▷   Understand the basic approach of this book

▷   Define what a business is and the main reason for control

▷   Describe the main features of the different sectors of the industry

▷   Describe the various activities of the financial control office.

What's a business?

Now we need to look at the nature of business and the hospitality industry in particular. We use the word 'business' here to mean any type of workplace, whether profit-making or not. Three definitions of a business are:

▷   'An industrial or commercial concern which exists to have dealings in the manufacture or purchase of goods for sale or the sale of a service'

▷   'A business invests in buildings and equipment and pays people to work in order to make more profit for the owners of the business'

▷   As above but 'makes money in order to fulfil some type of charitable purpose'.

These have been put together from a variety of sources but do give a broad outline of what a business is about. To decide which of these three is most appropriate to your area we need to look in more detail at the characteristics of the different sectors. But before that, let's look at the industry as a whole.

About hospitality and tourism

We have taken the broadest definition of hospitality – including not just hotels and catering but also tourism and leisure.

The hospitality and tourism industry is estimated to be worth about £6.4 billion pounds to the UK economy (*Caterer & Hotelkeeper*, 22 March 2001, p. 34). It employs 6.4% of the workforce which is about 1.9 million people. In terms of government we are 'looked after' by the Department of Culture, Media and Sport (DCMS) although there's input from the Department of Trade and Industry (DTI) as well.

The HCIMA yearbook is a good source of industry statistics and sources, if you are a member. The 2001 edition (pages 21-32) says that there are about 300,000 outlets, about 70% of which are profit-making and 30% non-profit. This means about 9,000 million 'meals' in a year! The industry is divided principally into hotels (61,000, though a lot more are thought to be unregistered – for instance small bed-and-breakfast establishments), catering in education (34,000), pubs (55,000) and restaurants, of which there are about 29,000 cafés and takeaways.

Some years are very good for the business although when we have a national economic crisis (or world recession, foot-and-mouth disease, very bad summer weather, for instance) this can have a widespread impact. In these circumstances people travel less in and to the UK and so don't spend money, which means businesses can afford fewer staff. This means unemployment or shortened hours which in turn makes staff less willing to spend their own money on meals, travel, entertainment and so on. The whole economy suffers if hospitality is down.

Overall features of the industry

Commercial versus non-commercial

The industry tends to be divided into commercial (hotels, restaurants, fast food, pubs, transport catering, clubs, cruise ships, outside catering, tour operators) and subsidized (hospitals, prisons, education, armed services). Commercial businesses need to persuade people to buy their products – and since this relies on disposable income customer make choices on whether or not they will spend their money on these.

On the other hand, where there is a captive market (prison, factory, airline or school meals, for instance) then you need to keep your customers happy for different reasons, whilst operating within imposed financial constraints.

Hours of operation

For many it's a 24-hour business which means that there are features and problems which don't affect many other types of industry, which may well operate on a five day, 39-hour week and be closed on public holidays.

Other industries (and government as well, perhaps) don't always recognize the particular problems that emerge here and the costs involved. For instance, they may see a motorway service area only in the middle of the day, forgetting it needs to be open all night to provide toilets, meals and petrol, or that nurses, hotel porters and crew on a ship are on duty all night and need to be fed.

Types of industry

There are different types of industry within hospitality too. There's production (like manufacturing – for instance in a kitchen), retail (a bar is like a shop) and service (restaurants, rooms).

Perishability

One principal feature is perishability – if the product isn't sold today then it can't be sold tomorrow. A room in a hotel, a cabin on a cruise ship, a place on a tour or a ride on a big-dipper are all examples. The raw materials may also be perishable (such as fresh food) which means that if they are not sold then they could be wasted. Businesses may be also very seasonal – a pub in a student area, a cruise line, a summer resort – may all have peaks and troughs in trade at different times of year, as well as on different days of the week.

Features of the different sectors

Here are some features listed for a number of different sectors – you may well be able to think of a lot more.

Hotels

Multi-unit and multi-product – rooms, food and beverage, leisure and subsidiary services. Food and beverage may be restaurants, cafés, carveries, banqueting, conferences, room service, lounge, club, vending. Hotels vary in size, in standard, in facilities offered and in length of stay. We also include in this sector simple bed-and breakfast or budget sector accommodation where few facilities are offered, and apart-hotels that are apartment blocks with hotel-style services available.

Here you see the multi-industry approach – production, retail and service all appear in one department or another. A restaurant may have all three. This complexity means that there will be many differently-skilled staff and systems.

'Front of house' means the operating units (sales to customers) whereas 'back of house' is all the support services the customer doesn't see, such as kitchens, maintenance and accounting.

Resorts

These are even more complex – like hotels but with extensive leisure facilities and services. Some of the staff, such as sports managers, may not even consider themselves as being part of 'hospitality'. This can mean issues regarding conflict of interest or lack of awareness of guest needs.

You can often find inclusive packages being sold for resorts – the price you pay includes a room, meals, sports and perhaps beauty therapy as well.

Residential homes and hostels

These are similar to hotels in concept but provide long-stay accommodation and limited facilities, albeit with a 'home-from-home' approach. Many have only a few rooms (such as residential homes for the elderly) and so control problems are limited. The opposite is the university campus which may have hundreds of bedrooms, perhaps on several sites, where problems with theft and damage can be enormous.

If they offer meals (and some offer three meals a day) then they will be allowed a certain amount of money to cater for them. This subsidy can be quite low if funding is given by educational or social service departments.

Restaurants (and cafés and fast food)

A whole range of different types of service – from haute cuisine with full silver service to takeaways. They are often strongly branded being either owned or franchised and may be themed around either a product such as pizza or coffee, or a style, such as Japanese.

They can have very strong control systems where the slightest variation is noticeable (e.g. fast food). This is essential if they are situated in very expensive locations such as high streets and shopping malls.

The food may be prepared from scratch with all raw ingredients or bought in fully prepared, depending on the type. Some menus and dishes are very complex whereas others may be very simple, depending on the type of restaurant.

One growing area is for cafés in shops. Although traditional department stores have always had restaurants you'll now find outlets in bookshops, supermarkets or clothes shops. They may well use this to advertise their own products, such as own-label food or china so although there's still a profit motive this may be for the whole store not just the catering outlet.

Pubs

A great variety dependent on location – they may serve a small village, where they have an important social function, or be in the middle of a city. They tend to be either 'beverage led' or 'food led'. Many modern pubs also include additional facilities such as entertainment or playbarns, to attract particular sectors of the market, or be themed ('Irish' bars, for instance).

Pubs have a lot of cash, drink and cigarettes and also a traditionally itinerant and low-paid workforce which make them particularly prone to control problems.

Cruise ships

These are floating resort hotels – with the added complication of a ship's crew and the need to find supplies in a variety of locations. Some of the larger ships have well over 1,000 staff and two or three thousand passengers – an enormous number of people to accommodate, feed and entertain.

The package that is offered to guests is usually 'all inclusive' with up to seven meals a day and most entertainment being included in the price. Although this reduces the potential problems with collecting payment it can mean very tight cost controls are needed. There are also logistical issues regarding supplies if a ship is away from port for several days.

Staff tend to work seven days a week for the period of their contract, which may be six or seven months away from home. The hospitality staff (as opposed to the ship's operating crew) may be multi-skilled and expected to help out in a range of areas.

Transport catering

Rail, inflite, motorway service areas (MSAs) – as well as cruise lines above. You often have potential for a captive market here (although you can just be competing against customers bringing their own supplies) so you need to ensure that you offer value for money. The pricing may be very tight and so strict controls are essential if the business is to make any sort of profit. There's a tendency now to offer branded products in MSAs and on rail stations.

Trains may have to offer trolley as well as buffet services, and planes a variety of food types, to satisfy differently-priced categories of traveller. If their customers are 'captive' (even if just for a few hours) then they may also need to cater for a range of diets.

Leisure centres

The main function of these is to provide sporting facilities – pool, gym, squash courts and perhaps therapies with catering as a minor part of the operation. Some units may only have vending machines whereas others may have much more extensive catering – it depends on the location, the space and the clientele.

Since the focus is on the leisure facilities there may be little revenue from catering which may mean it running at a loss or providing a very limited service.

Contract catering

A wide range is found here – from catering for residential schools, oil rigs or universities to office staff in a large city. Often these will have a secondary purpose in keeping the 'customers' together and encouraging good behaviour and timekeeping. Although the prices tend to be low the customers may still be very demanding in terms of quality and menu choice and may be very aware of healthy eating trends.

You may well be competing with customers bringing in their own food or going elsewhere to eat so you need to ensure a good product and service to attract and keep your customers. More than one type of catering may also be offered as part of a single contract, such as a directors' dining room, main restaurant, coffee shop and vending. In multi-unit sites, or where there is a food court (lots of small units in one area, suitable for high volumes) there's a trend towards using high-street brands as well as in-house brand names.

Contracts can be either 'cost plus' where all costs plus a fee are charged to the client or 'fixed price' where there is a greater incentive for the operator to control costs and maximize revenues. Performance guarantees need to be put in place so that standards are maintained and costs don't rise to unacceptable levels. Others may operate on a 'nil cost' basis where the contractor does not earn a fee but gains their revenue from the discounts negotiated with suppliers – you need very high volumes and very tight cost control for this to be effective.

Contract caterers are often able to supplement the basic facility with 'hospitality' services that typically are directors' dining rooms, meeting room catering and special functions. They usually have a separate pricing structure and are additional to the standard product – and so are more profitable. Other services now being added to the contract are non-catering items such as laundry, cleaning services and shops. The length of a contract can vary depending on the type operation and the amount of investment each side wishes to make.

Function or event catering

These offer outside catering at events such as sports tournaments and tends to be a one-off event, run at a temporary venue (such as in a marquee) with logistical problems such as having to supply all equipment as well as staff and food and drink. This may range from corporate hospitality at a sporting event to a hot-dog stall at a country fair.

There will be a small core staff but many will be employed on a casual basis for a single event, which means that their motivation for working is more to do with money than job satisfaction and career prospects. There can be lots of opportunities to cheat both the customer and operator, with a lot of high value items in transit.

Clubs

These may be licensed, where an individual runs them, or registered, where a committee runs them. They often offer cut-price services in return for an annual membership fee. If run by a committee then they may be not-for-profit, so the main purpose is to provide a service for members and to cover costs. Without a professional management approach there may be losses that the committee isn't aware of.

Hospitals

Catering and domestic services may both be run by the same contractor who may be an in-house team or an outside contractor. There are lots of issues affecting the operation with the health of patients being of paramount importance, despite very limited budgets. Hospital staff and visitors also need to be serviced, with different needs from patients who are there for 24 hours a day, often for a long period. Apart from these commercial aspects, the main operations (cleaning and patient feeding) tend to be regarded as cost-only operations.

Education

Catering can range from school meals (often run by a local authority caterer) to residential services in a university. Contract caterers may be employed to run on-site catering in partnership with the college or university management, so as to bring in professional expertise and purchasing power.

Volumes can be enormous – some schools may be serving 1,000 lunches a day and colleges even more. There may be a captive market (for instance in a boarding school) but often caterers are competing with customers bringing their own food from home. Prices tend to be low and so cost control is crucial.

Prison catering

Food is an important part of prison life and can be central to morale, and therefore good behaviour. Budgets are very limited but again three meals a day have to be supplied, as well as drinks and snacks. One of the other benefits to prisoners is that they may have the opportunity to work in the kitchens (saving on staffing costs) which develops their skills and helps them gain employment when they are released.

Tour operators

We tend to think of these as always offering accommodation, but packages may also be a day trip to a tourist destination, a theatre-plus-dinner outing or a day at a sporting event. Here the hospitality may be very simple or of a very high standard, such as a day at the races where a champagne lunch is offered.

Package holidays can be just travel and accommodation or may include meals and excursions as well. Although tour operators are more about organization than unit management they still need to be aware of customer needs, of pricing techniques and the importance of forecasting.

Attractions

These may also be very complex and offer a variety of types of operation – the attraction itself, a shop, café, picnic areas, vending, ice cream stalls and so on. They can be very seasonal – weekends and school holiday times providing the vast majority of their visitors – which means specific problems in staffing and purchasing of goods. Again there may be retail and service elements involved.

Forces catering

Although these have modernized considerably in recent years there are still separate 'messes' for different ranks, necessitating different standards of service. Budgets are limited despite the catering staff having to provide three meals a day for what may be very physically-active, hungry consumers often in remote locations and in transit between camps.

The importance of control

Before we look at the basics of finance we need to look why control is important to the business. If the different aspects of the business – revenues, expenses and assets – can be effectively managed, or 'controlled', then we can maximize profit (or, in the case of the non-profit sectors, break even or minimize subsidies).

This means that the business is more secure – and so is your job. Better financial results lead to increased wages, job security, company growth and hence better career prospects. Also, your wages mean that you contribute to the local economy by spending in shops and leisure facilities, and the taxes you pay help the country as a whole.

The main aspects of control are as folows (adapted from Davis, Lockwood & Stone, 1998).

Planning

▷   Company strategy and policies for the business

Operations

▷   Purchasing

▷   Receiving, storage and issue

▷   Preparation (including rooms)

▷   Selling the product or service

▷   Receiving payment

Management

▷ Efficient systems

▷ Physical controls

▷ Supervision

▷ Identification of problems and revising of systems

and also external audit which is a legal requirement for all large businesses.

All these areas involve people – and people don't always act as efficiently as they should for a variety of reasons (some of which we'll look at in the different chapters). As a result there is potential for:

▷ Wastage due to inefficiency

▷ Theft in some form or another.

In other words – there are ALWAYS control problems – but it is the manager's job to minimize these so as to maximize the profit (or minimize the costs) for the business and hopefully then improve their own salary and career prospects.

The main overall ways that these are done are:

▷ Separation of duties

▷ Awareness of systems and people

▷ Measurement

▷ Awareness of risk.

Attitudes to theft

First, think about *your* attitude to theft. Do you see small 'fiddles' as a part of pay? If you are underpaid and overworked then staff may see these as being a legitimate part of their income. What about a manager – do they have the same attitude? And what if it's a high value item that goes missing – is there a cut-off point where theft is acceptable or not?

There's often a 'fine line' between what is a legitimate benefit and what is theft or fraud, and the interpretation can actually vary in different operations. The point is that there is a culture within the business that will either encourage or discourage theft, and this will come from the 'top down'. If you are a large business you may well have stringent rules about what you may or may not do – and all staff from the general manager down may not be able to take anything from the business.

However, if your boss sees it as one of the perks to take food (for instance) away then this will impact on you and your colleagues – if the boss can do it, then why not you? If you are inherently honest (as most people are) then it can be very difficult working in a culture where theft is ignored or worse, actively encouraged. Trust is crucial, but so is stringent action when problems are identified.

TIP

No one is immune to dismissal for theft. Did you know that Escoffier and Ritz were sacked from the Savoy early last century for £15,000 of fraud?

Attitudes can also vary between countries and cultures. The customers and workforce in hospitality are international and the successful manager needs to recognize that this may mean different attitudes towards both the product and control – what is acceptable in one culture isn't in another.

Types of theft

There are two main types – theft and fraud – and we are covering both in this book.

Theft is stealing of physical items (including cash)

Fraud is using systems to divert money out of the business.

There's a general opinion that theft is committed by staff and fraud by managers and administrators, but this isn't always the case. It usually depends on opportunity.

Why do people steal?

People steal for lots of reasons but there's usually a combination of:

personal need + opportunity + attitude

Need is often because of financial issues. These can be due to genuine poverty or to self-induced problems such as debt, addiction or a desire to appear richer than you are.

Opportunity is how easy it is to thieve – which is where you come in. If you can reduce the opportunity then you cut out one of the three motivators.

Attitude is partly due to the ethics of the business (which we mentioned earlier) but also of the individual. Some people aren't honest and will try to steal; others will only steal if tempted or provoked. Attitudes can change if the individual feels let down by the employer – somebody who is overlooked for promotion, bored in their job (so stealing becomes a challenge) or bullied by their boss may well take 'revenge' by trying to steal company property.

Stakeholders

We've talked about the basics of control and why it's important to you – but it's relevant to other people too. These are the 'stakeholders' of the business – and may be interested in different things and for different reasons.

Here are some of them:

Staff (including you) want their wages paid, secure jobs, good working conditions and possibly career prospects.

Managers want the same and perhaps also an annual bonus if related to success.

Customers want to have their needs satisfied, and more.

Suppliers want to make sure they will be paid too, and that the business will grow and continue to provide them with a market for their goods and services.

Banks and building societies may have lent money and want to make sure that it (and the interest) will be paid.

The Government wants its taxes paid!

Owners want a return on their investment, both now and in the future.

Here's something for you to do: think about who the stakeholders are in your organization. Are there others than these quoted above (for instance, if you work in a hospital, what about visitors and patients)?

Organizational structures

The final part objective of this chapter is to have an overview of the organization and see how the different departments fit together. In particular we will concentrate on the financial control (or accounts) department and look at the responsibilities of the different areas. Obviously this will vary in different sectors and also according to the type of accounts they do.

As the most complex type of land-based operation is the leisure hotel (cruise ships can have crew as well but often simplify some of their operations) we'll use that as an example. Figure 1.1 shows a typical management structure for a large property:

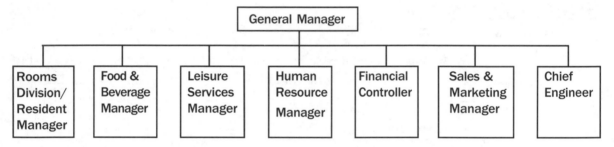

Figure 1.1 Executive Committee of a Leisure Hotel

Typically the top managers form the 'executive committee' and are responsible for several departments, each with their own managers, supervisors and so on.

However, new structures are often found now which relate more to the type of responsibility rather than the department – so a revenue manager can be responsible not just for rooms but perhaps for food and beverage (F&B) revenue too, in a smaller property. If rooms and F&B are still separate then a revenue manager may look after all room sales – from selling through yield management/reservations to check in and out. There may not be a great deal of difference to the traditional Rooms Division but the focus is very much on maximizing revenues (but does this take the emphasis away from costs?- we'll see in later chapters).

Financial control or accounts department

What do they do?

They look after all the money! This is partly to do with cash but they also maximize revenues and minimize costs by a range of control processes that are divided out among the different sections.

You'll see a large range of job titles and in a big property (around 1000 rooms) you may find up to 40 people involved in the various areas. It can depend on the amount of computerization they have (computers DO save work here) but also whether the property is *self-accounting* or has *centralized accounts*.

Centralized accounting

This means that very few of the accounts are prepared at the property and almost all information is transmitted to a head office where it is processed by specialist staff. This approach has grown in recent years with the rapid rise in technology, which means easy transmission of data and is particularly appropriate for fairly simple operations such as lodges and fast-food restaurants.

For instance, when the till system (whatever the sector) is closed down at the end of each day the information on sales, cash received, credit cards and products sold can all be automatically downloaded. When goods are delivered the details are punched in another terminal of the central computer, and again this data is transmitted.

There is little need for a control department because all information is simple and very tightly managed. The management team will then have to perform what's called a 'self-audit' by completing questionnaires to check a range of procedures daily and periodically, which ensures that checks are taking place. It's also very cheap to operate which means lower costs and hence lower prices for customers.

Self- accounting

Here the property does ALL its own accounts – gathers all the revenues including all debts, pays all invoices, produces final profit and loss and balance sheets and then pays its own taxes. Independent businesses are almost all like this, but so are some large properties that are part of a group, often for tax reasons. This type of property needs a lot of control staff, in the various areas.

Here it's essential that all the responsibilities are segregated so that there's no possibility of fraud – so for instance the person who receives the cheques in the mail doesn't pay them into the bank, and somebody else has to check them off against debtors. This is time-consuming and expensive but essential from an audit perspective.

A variation on this is that you do most of these tasks but a few (such as credit control, purchasing or reconciliation of taxes) are handled by head office. This is called 'semi-self-accounting'.

▶▶ **ACTIVITY**

Do you have an accounting office – either on-site or at head office? Talk to the controller and find out what type of accounts they have.

Here's what all the people do in a self-accounting unit:

Financial controller

The manager of the department who is responsible for all the activities as well as the people. In a self-accounting unit he or she may be called a '*financial director*' and have legal as well as managerial responsibilities. They have to ensure that all controls ('*audits*') are performed and that the accounts give a 'true and fair view' of the financial position at the end of each month. They are often formally qualified in accounting.

Assistant controller

Second in command – in a big unit may be the person who actually manages all the day-to-day business.

Revenue controller (or 'income auditor')

This person checks that all the revenues that have been processed via the various departments are accurate and that everything that has been consumed has been paid for.

Credit controller and Sales ledger staff

She or he manages the sales ledger (or 'accounts receivable') which records all the debtors. They approve all requests for credit, check and process invoices, chase customers who don't pay and then process payments. They may also process charge card and company credit card payments.

Purchase ledger (accounts payable)

Checks and pays all the invoices due to suppliers for goods, for services, utilities and to governments.

General cashier

The general cashier checks all the cash that has been received from a variety of sources, banks it and may reconcile all bank statements with the assistant controller. Cash includes cheques, credit cards and foreign exchange. They will also check the various floats in the unit with a member of security.

Food and beverage controller

May have equal status with the assistant controller and is responsible for lots of staff in the purchasing and stores area. They check all aspects of food and beverage, from purchasing through delivery, storage and issue to departments. They are also responsible for all the stocktaking (inventory) and hence the calculation of cost of sales.

Computer services

Sometimes reports here or may report to Front office or direct to the GM. This is an increasingly important job with responsibility for all hardware and software. In a smaller operation these responsibilities may be held by the Controller as well and form part of their job description.

Payroll clerk

Checks all the timesheets (manual or technological) and processes payments to staff. In the past they would also hand out wage packets but nowadays most staff are paid directly into a bank account which reduces costs and security problems. They need to know a lot about the legal aspects of employment – maternity and sick pay, for instance, can be very complicated.

Month end

You should now appreciate some of the complexity of the control area and the types of jobs that people do. Finally a brief word about 'month end'. This is the period around the last day of the month when all transactions have to be processed up to date, when the stocktaking (inventories) are done and when lots of additional calculations take place in order to produce the final accounts. It forms a key part of the overall financial control framework. We'll look a bit more at some of these in the next chapter.

Accounts staff get a bit stressed at month end as all data has to be processed to a very tight schedule in order to produce the 'trial balance' (a list of totals of all the account codes) and then draft accounts. Be nice to them please!

▶▶ ACTIVITY ▬▬▬▬▬▬▬▬▬▬▬▬▬▬▬

Are all these functions performed in your unit or are some outsourced to another area or company? Payroll, for instance, is often processed outside the company because of the complexity of the laws and the need for sophisticated computer software as a result.

Summary

Here we have looked at the basic concept of control – prevention of wastage and theft and why it's important to you. We've also looked at some of the main features of the industry and of the different sectors. There has been a review of the organization of the business and of the accounts office, and of the jobs that are required in order to produce accurate results for you and other managers. Many of the techniques you'll practise in this book are relevant to most or all sectors, so hopefully they will be useful to you both now and in the future.

Remember though that you always need to think of the customer first – that's your job as a manager. In this book we're going to show that you can serve both the customer and manage the financial aspects at the same time.

Quiz

▷   What are the main features of a residential home?

▷   What different types of contract catering are there?

▷   What's the difference between centralized and self-accounting?

▷   What does the accounts payable (purchase ledger) clerk do?

▷   What's the definition of a business?

See if you know the answers. Then go back to the relevant section in the text and see if you were correct.

2

Understanding management reports

▼
▼
▼
▼
▼

Profit & Loss Report ◀

Performance analysis ◀

The Balance Sheet ◀

Adjustments to accounts ◀

Introduction

In this chapter we'll look at the main type of report that you will need to help you manage your area better – the Profit and Loss Report. For different departments you'll see reports that include not only monetary but also percentages for the actual amounts, the amount that was budgeted, and the difference between them. Later in the chapter we'll see how to use these.

There are also statements used by the general manager – a summary Profit and Loss (P&L) and then the Balance Sheet which is important when managing stocks, cash and debtors as well as showing the total value and stability of the business. In order to know how all these accounts are put together we will also examine the activities that need to take place at the end of each month.

So by the end of this chapter you should be able to:

▷   Identify different items that appear in a Profit & Loss report

▷   Calculate profits for a simple business

▷   Calculate variances and percentages

▷   Assemble a balance sheet

▷   Calculate accruals, prepayments and depreciation.

Some of this may seem a bit 'dry' but you do need to understand the basics of accounts before you can use the information to help you. So please persevere with the 'theory' and then the next Chapter will have more practical applications which will seem more relevant to your job, either now or in the future.

Before we look at the P&L we need to clarify what is meant by 'financial reports'. There are two types produced for a commercial business – generally classified as 'financial accounts' and 'management accounts'.

Financial accounts are produced yearly (and half-yearly) and are formal, official records that have to be submitted for legal reasons to tax and company authorities. For a large company they may also be known as 'published accounts'. There are a lot of rules as to how these are presented and some of these will be covered further in Chapter 10 of this book.

Management accounts are used within the business by the managers to help them be more effective – so they are designed to suit the manager's needs (in theory!). They are usually produced every month (or period) which may be a calendar month (so 12 a year) or four weeks (13 a year). Some businesses also have two four-week months and then a five-week month (so 12 in a year again) although this structure can be a bit awkward to manage.

Now let's look at the main accounting statement that a manager needs – the 'P&L'. (By the way – you can't get profit AND loss together, can you? But it's always called this – and always abbreviated to P&L, which is what we will call it too).

Profit & Loss Report

This is a statement of the revenue and expenditure (also called *sales* and *costs* – the terms tend to be interchangeable) and one minus the other equals profit or loss. We try to avoid using the word 'income' as in the UK it means what we earn and in the USA can mean net profit.

A department which has sales is called an 'operating department' and is a 'profit centre'. You can also have statements for departments that don't have sales – such as maintenance – these are called 'cost centres'. As we saw in Chapter 1, some businesses such as hospital catering may only have costs.

So, what is 'profit'? These definitions come from a variety of sources:

▷ Excess of revenue over expenditure

▷ Excess of revenue over expenditure

▷ Excess of sales over related costs

▷ Reward for the entrepreneur (owner).

You can also look at it as being a sharing out of the sales, if you have them. Figure 2.1 is an example where the 'cake' represents the sales and the slices the costs and profit.

Generally the most profitable type of business is accommodation although the costs of running a building can be high. Profits can be very volatile unless it is part of another business, such as spare bedrooms in a farmhouse run as a B&B. Profitability is relative though – what is good in one sector may be modest in another, and some locations are more profitable than others.

Figure 2.1   Costs and profit

Small businesses

For a simple operation such as a pub, a small restaurant or a bed-and-breakfast you might not need a complicated report – just one that shows you where your money has come from, and gone to. There's no point in wasting time doing extensive accounts if you don't need them (but you DO need to do some accounts for tax reasons).

For 'Billie's B&B' there isn't a need for complicated accounts – the owners' time is better spent with their customers – so here's the sort of statement that is useful to them:

	(£)
Sales	20,000
Less cost of sales	(2,000)
Equals gross profit	18,000
Less payroll	(3,900)
Less other controllable expenses	(2,400)
Equals gross operating profit	11,700
Less fixed costs	(5,200)
Net profit	6,500

Before we go through line-by-line a couple of things to tell you. First, you'll see that the figures are laid out in columns. Accounts are always done like this as they are easier for you to read and to do the adding and subtracting if this has to be done manually (and spreadsheets, if you use them, are columnar too). The figures are always 'right justified' so that the thousands are always in the same place – again it's easier to read. The titles ('sales' and so on) are left justified although sometimes you may see them indented. For a P&L you don't need to show pence, just round pounds, although when we come to ratios this changes.

Another thing that is easy to read is using brackets for minus figures – subtracting is quicker like this than reading a small dash sign. The only problem is that some spreadsheet packages don't have brackets set up automatically so you may need to do this (see Chapter 9). Lastly, you underline above a sub-total and below a total so you can see that those are summary figures.

By the way, in Europe all these reports are produced net of tax (Value Added Tax – VAT) which belongs to the government and not the business. In countries with sales and purchases taxes this may be handled differently.

What do all the titles mean?

Here's a list:

Revenue (sales)

All the sales that you make to customers – what they pay for the goods and services they buy from you. They are recorded on the day that the meal is eaten, the room occupied, the flight taken – NOT on the day that they are actually paid for. We'll talk more about payment in Chapter 7.

Cost of sales (CoS)

The cost of the raw materials used to make the meals and drinks – all the stocks that are used – and also in hotels the cost of telephone units for guest calls and the cost of guest dry cleaning. All other costs such as linen or paper appear elsewhere.

Gross profit (GP)

Sales less cost of sales.

Payroll

All the cost of employing staff – their salaries or wages, overtime and all the benefits associated (also known as 'on cost') such as national insurance, holiday pay, uniforms and meals.

Controllable expenses

All other general expenses used in the operation that can be managed and controlled on a daily basis (so yes to paper napkins and electricity but no to rent – see below).

Gross operating profit (GOP)

Profit from all items that can be controlled effectively within the unit.

Fixed charges

Rent and rates, depreciation, insurance, loan interest – the 'overheads' of the business. These are the items that can't really be controlled on a day-to-day basis. They are called 'fixed' because they don't change very often – and don't rise and fall with the level of business.

Net profit (NP or NOP)

What you have left.

Note: if you look at an accounting textbook, or see some final accounts for a small business, you may see two further lines – 'less tax' and then 'net profit after tax'. We're not covering tax in this book – it's far too complicated – so ignore it please for now. An accountant is the best person to help you with tax matters as it's a specialist area and errors can be very expensive.

▶▶ **ACTIVITY**

Do you have a P&L for your unit? Ask to see it and see how complicated it is.

Larger businesses

Most operations, however, are bigger than this with several different areas or departments. A large pub may have two different bars and food, an attraction will have a shop and a café as well as entrance fees, hospital services both catering and cleaning services and so on – so they need more information than shown above.

The managers of these different areas need to know how well or how badly their area is performing – and so need their own financial reports. Although you know how many customers you have, and whether they are spending lots of money, you may not always be aware of all the costs associated with this. For instance, if you pay staff overtime it may be far more expensive than hiring in a part-timer for a day. A good manager needs to know everything about the financial aspects as well as the operational ones.

Responsibility accounting

Having your own departmental statement is called responsibility accounting and is linked to a formal structure of departmental statements called the Uniform System of Accounts. The most well-known is the one for hotels ('Lodging', in American terms – abbreviated to USAL) but there are other versions for other sectors such as clubs, hospitals and restaurants. Using these means that every unit has the same approach to finance and can be compared against each other (or one business to another) and managers will always understand (in theory!) what appears where.

Departmental statements

The separate statements for each department look a little like Figure 2.2 (they may well be adapted a little to suit different companies).

This month									
Actual	%	Budget	%	Variance	%	Last year	%		
									Sales
									Cost of sales
									Gross profit
									Payroll
									Expenses
									Departmental profit

Figure 2.2   Layout for departmental statements

What's shown here is only half the statement – on the right-hand side will be a similar set of columns for the Year to Date. The Cost of Sales, payroll and expenses are deducted as before.

You can see that there are 'Actual', 'Budget', 'Variance' and 'Last Year' columns. The actual is what did happen and the budget what was planned (there's more of this in Chapter 6, *Forecasting*) – and the variance the difference between them (it's always calculated to budget so if actual sales were less than budget it would show as a minus). The 'Last year' column shows the previous year's actual figure.

These all allow comparisons to be made between what was expected and what actually happened. For instance, if sales are up then costs should be up too and so should profits. You can look just at money but considering these as a percentage can also help (more on this below).

The rows only show the titles here as well – they would actually include a long list of all the different categories such as types of sales and costs (known as 'account codes' as they all have a separate code number in the accounting system that helps assign them). For instance, if this was used for an attraction's café the sales section would show the different types of food such as drinks, sandwiches, ice cream, crisps and so on. The expenses will include items like plastic cups and cleaning materials.

If it's a statement for a cost centre then it wouldn't have the first three rows – only the payroll, expenses and departmental cost total.

▶▶   **ACTIVITY** ━━━━━━━━━━━━━━━━━━━━━━━━━━━━━━━━━━━━━

Do you have access to departmental report? If you don't, then ask if you can look at one. Is your statement similar to the example above? You can see the type of headings that appear and the ratios that are calculated. Does this statement actually help you, or the manager of that area, do their job properly, or could improvements be made?

The general manager then receives a statement that consolidates or accumulates all these departmental statements together – this is known as the 'front page P&L'. It's designed to fit on one page so that it can be read easily and so summarizes many of the figures – it doesn't include all the detail that your departmental statement would have. Again there's a current month and then a year-to-date set of columns. Figure 2.3 is an example for a hotel.

The top sections summarize all the operating departments and then the others, the cost centres which service the whole establishment, appear after the DOP line.

	Actual	%	Budget	%	Variance	%	Last year	%
Sales								
Rooms								
Food								
Beverage								
Other								
Total sales								
Gross profits								
Rooms								
Food								
Beverage								
Other								
Total gross profit (GP)								
Payroll								
Benefits								
Total payroll								
Expenses – departmental								
Departmental operating profit (DOP)								
Undistributed operating expenses								
Administration								
Energy								
Repairs & maintenance								
Sales & marketing								
Gross operating profit (GOP)								
Fixed charges								
Net profit (NP)								

Figure 2.3 Layout for 'front page' statements

Now here's a chance for you to do a small exercise to practise putting the numbers together. This is a pub with rooms, so please do separate departments (even though they are very small) and the front page P&L. We've included budget figures so you can calculate variances as well.

	Actual (£)	Budget (£)
Food & beverage sales	12,000	12,500
Cost of Sales	3,800	3,800
Accommodation sales	1,900	1,950
Wages – food and beverage	2,700	2,700
Employee benefits – food and beverage	500	500
Wages – accommodation	400	400
Employee benefits – accommodation	80	80
Food and beverage expenses	1,600	1,600
Accommodation expenses	200	200
Administration expenses	1,100	1,100
Rates	500	500
Maintenance costs	100	100
Depreciation	1,400	1,400

▼
▼

TIP

It's often easiest to set out all the titles first and then put in the numbers. Lastly you do the addition and subtraction. Another tip is to tick off every number and title that you use from the question when you use them in the answer. You'll then know you haven't forgotten anything.

Here's the answer:

Pub P&L

	Actual (£)	Actual (%)	Budget (£)	Budget (%)	Variance (£)	Variance (%)
Food and beverage						
Sales	12,000	100.0	12,500	100.0	(500)	(4.0)
Cost of sales	(3,800)	(31.7)	(3,800)	(30.4)	0	0.0
Gross profit	8,200	68.3	8,700	69.6	(500)	(5.7)
Payroll	(2,700)	(22.5)	(2,700)	(21.6)	0	0.0
Benefits	(500)	(4.2)	(500)	(4.0)	0	0.0
Dept. expenses	(1,600)	(13.3)	(1,600)	(12.8)	0	0.0
Net profit	3,400	28.3	3,900	31.2	(500)	(12.8)

Accommodation

	Actual (£)	(%)	Budget (£)	(%)	Variance (£)	(%)
Sales	1,900	100.0	1,950	100.0	(50)	(2.6)
Payroll	(400)	(21.1)	(400)	(20.5)	0	0.0
Benefits	(80)	(4.2)	(80)	(4.1)	0	0.0
Dept. expenses	(200)	(10.5)	(200)	(10.3)	0	0.0
Net profit	1,220	64.2	1,270	65.1	(50)	(3.9)
Administration						
Admin. expenses	1,100	7.9	1,100	7.6	0	0.0
Maintenance	100	0.7	100	0.7	0	0.0
Total	1,200	8.6	1,200	8.3	0	0.0
Fixed charges						
Rates	500	3.6	500	3.5	0	0.0
Depreciation	1,400	10.1	1,400	9.7	0	0.0
Total	1,900	13.7	1,900	13.1	0	0.0

	Actual (£)	(%)	Budget (£)	(%)	Variance (£)	(%)
Front page P&L						
Sales – F&B	12,000	86.3	12,500	86.5	(500)	(4.0)
Sales – Accomodation	1,900	13.7	1,950	13.5	(50)	(2.6)
	13,900	100.0	14,450	100.0	(550)	(3.8)
Cost of sales	(3,800)	(27.3)	(3,800)	(26.3)	0	0.0
Gross profit	10,100	72.7	10,650	73.7	(550)	(5.2)
Dept. payroll	(3,100)	(22.3)	(3,100)	(21.5)	0	0.0
Dept. benefits	(580)	(4.2)	(580)	(4.0)	0	0.0
Dept. expenses	(1,800)	(12.9)	(1,800)	(12.5)	0	0.0
Dept. profit	4,620	33.2	5,170	35.8	(550)	(10.6)
Admin costs	(1,200)	(8.6)	(1,200)	(8.3)	0	0.0
Gross operating profit	3,420	24.6	3,970	27.5	(550)	(13.9)
Fixed charges	(1,900)	(13.7)	(1,900)	(13.1)	0	0.0
Net profit	1,520	10.9	2,070	14.3	(550)	(26.6)

*The percentages in the figures will be explained a bit further down.

Performance analysis

Now that we've had time to look at this main statement, what do we DO with it? What should you, as a manager or supervisor, use these for?

It is the departmental reports that are likely to be of most value to you. You can:

▷   Compare actual to budget, and to last year, in money

▷   Compare these by different percentages

▷   Compare average spends

▷   Look at productivity

▷   Look at costs per customer.

Variances

First you can just look at the variance between actual and budget. Variances can be good as well as bad – but it depends on whose perspective you look from! A high cost of labour may be bad for profits but good for customers, so you do need to find the balance between good service and good cost.

Why don't we just look at variances, though? Look at the F&B department results for the pub with rooms that we did before. You can see that there's a big variance in money terms between the actual and the budget profits although the sales show only a small variance. The tendency is JUST to look at money without seeing where the problem lies. Is it revenue or is it costs? But… if revenues are down then surely costs should be too? If you only look at variances in money amounts then you don't know if the costs are right for this level of revenues.

Now you can compare one percentage to another. You'll see that the budget cost percentage was lower than the actual but that the budget and actual payroll amounts are equal. That means that there's potentially a problem – the cost amount of payroll should have been reduced so that the percentage stays the same. (You can also use this if the actual is higher than budget.)

You'll see that the percentage of profit to sales is worse for the actual than the budget so, although the sales are up, profits haven't risen as much. If you look at the costs percentages you'll see where the problem is (cost of sales). This tells you that you've a problem in that area, which wouldn't have been evident if you'd only looked at the totals.

You can also look at the average amount you get from each customer and the average costs, and see how much profit is generated. (You'll see how to calculate these in later Chapters). If the pub served 3,000 customers then the average spend on F&B would be £4.00.

What's a percentage?

(Just in case you've not done them for a long time.) A percentage is the proportion of one figure to another, expressed in parts of 100. So half an apple is 50% of the total and a quarter is 25%. For control purposes we normally add one decimal point (tenths of a percentage) so half is expressed as 50.0% and a third as 33.3%.

We'll see how to calculate these a bit further on.

The percentages for the Actual and Budget columns are all expressed to sales – so the GP percentage is the proportion of GP in money to the sales figure. The variance percentage for any item is the variance in money as a percentage of the budget.

TIP

Want to check if the percentages are correct? Add them up in the same way as you add the money amounts. So, on the front page, actual column, add 86.3+13.7 = 100, subtract 27.3=72.7 and so on all the way down to the net profit. This is called 'cross casting'.

So, who needs them?

Answer – the stakeholders of the organization who we discussed in Chapter 1 – management, staff, creditors, owners and so on. They all use ratios to compare one business to another, one unit to another, one month to another. Using ratios means that you can have a 'common size' for comparison, for instance:

▷   Seat turnover in one pizza restaurant to another

▷   Average room rate in a budget hotel compared to last year before they built the extension

▷   Meal cost per person from one hospital to another

▷   Profits from one pub chain to another

▷   Average bet in a casino

▷   Type of customers (called 'market segments' but you could also mean by age range).

It doesn't matter if one unit is twice the size of another – by using ratios you can make comparisons.

There are some 'key ratios' for revenue, cost, cash and stocks and productivity areas that we will look at later but you also need to be aware of overall profit (or cost) ratios, which we'll cover briefly now.

'Bottom line' results

At general manager and company level the emphasis is often very much on the 'bottom line'. This is always looked at in money terms but also, depending on the business and the sector, they may measure this in percentages, in amount per customer, or both. It may also be the GOP level rather than NOP – for instance a restaurant or hotel operated via management contract or franchise often have to pay a fee based on the achieved GOP. Other operations such as shops or cafés at an airport or in a shopping complex, may pay not a fixed rent but one based on sales (as a percentage) and occasionally on profits. This encourages the operator to be efficient in their control of costs and to optimize sales.

Why not try to calculate the percentages and average spends yourself? You can practise on the pub P&L, above. Then you can do the accommodation area – assume they sold 55 rooms. Lastly do the percentages for the front page P&L.

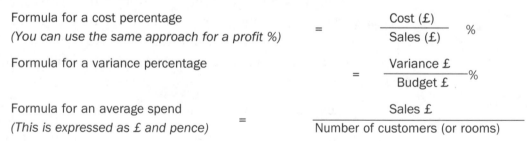

Formula for a cost percentage
(You can use the same approach for a profit %)

$$= \frac{\text{Cost (£)}}{\text{Sales (£)}} \%$$

Formula for a variance percentage

$$= \frac{\text{Variance £}}{\text{Budget £}} \%$$

Formula for an average spend
(This is expressed as £ and pence)

$$= \frac{\text{Sales £}}{\text{Number of customers (or rooms)}}$$

TIP

How to do a percentage:

Type the top figure in the formula into your calculator, hit the divide key, type in the bottom figure then hit the percentage key. This will give you the answer with the decimal point in the right place, so you don't need to bother with multiplying by 100.

For cost centres the percentage is calculated to the total sales of the business (so energy in a hotel is expressed as a percentage of total hotel sales).

The Balance Sheet

Now we need to look at the second main statement that is used by the unit to help manage the business. These may not appear in all operations – if your unit is part of a larger division or company then all these items below may be managed 'higher up'. Even if that is the case, however, it's useful for you to see how your actions in the area say of cash and stocks can affect the value of the business.

The balance sheet (BS) is a statement taken at a specific date (compared to the P&L which accumulated the figures over a period) – so it's often been described as a 'snapshot'. It's a report on the *assets* and *liabilities* of the unit, on the last day of the period. These can be either long-term (fixed) or short-term (current) in the way they behave.

A bit of accounting theory here – the concept of 'double entry book-keeping' was invented hundreds of years ago by a monk. You don't need to understand how it works, but the basic 'accounting equation' is that:

Everything that is OWNED (an asset) is matched by

Everything that is OWED (a liability)

And so the total of the ASSETS equals the total of the LIABILITIES.

Here's some examples you might be familiar with. 'Long term' means that they won't change much in a year whereas short-term ones often change daily. You'll see why they are split a bit later on.

Assets *(WE OWN)*

Fixed assets *(last more than a year)*

▷   Land & buildings

▷   Furniture, fixtures & equipment

▷   Vehicles

Long-term investments

▷   Investments (e.g. shares) in other companies

▷   Bank and Building Society (long-term) deposits

Current assets

▷   Bank balances (current accounts) and floats

▷   Stocks of food, drink and so on

▷   Debtors (people who owe us money – in some businesses may be called 'receivables')

▷   Prepayments (items paid for in advance – see below)

Liabilities   *(WE OWE)*

Current liabilities

▷   Creditors (people we owe money to, may be called 'payables')

▷   Accruals (things we have used but not yet paid for – more below)

▷   Bank overdraft (if you have one)

Fixed liabilities and capital

▷   Capital (the original investment in the business to start it up. It belongs to the owners so counts as a debt because, if the company were to close down, it should be repaid)

▷   Long-term loans such as mortgages

▷   Net profit (this is owed to the owners as their reward for the investment they put in)

▷   Drawings (money taken out of the business as profits by the owners)

You might have all of these or only some of them. You might just rent your building or equipment rather than own it, for instance, or you may only accept cash payments and so have no debtors. Now can you decide where some of these items might appear in the balance sheet:

Computer	Mortgage
Delivery van	Staff accommodation that is owned
Stocks of frozen food	Phone units used but not paid for
Amount owing from a customer	Overdraft
Yearly rental on coffee machine, paid in advance	
Amount owing to a supplier	

Here's the answer:

	Assets	Liabilities
Computer	✓	
Mortgage		✓
Delivery van	✓	
Staff accommodation that is owned	✓	
Stocks of frozen food	✓	
Phone units used but not paid for		✓
Yearly rental on coffee machine, paid in advance	✓	
Amount owing from a customer	✓	
Overdraft		✓
Amount owing to a supplier		✓

Did you get them right? Can you think of any more in your area?

Remembering that as Assets = Liabilities you can also see that all assets will also equal capital and other liabilities.

Please can you fill in the gaps so you can see how it works:

	Assets		Capital		Liabilities
A	£2,800	=	[ ]	+	£2,100
B	£285	=	£226	+	[ ]
C	£52,000	=	[ ]	+	£20,600
D	[ ]	=	£3400	+	£1,500

And the answer:

	Assets		Capital		Liabilities
A	£2,800	=	£700	+	£2,100
B	£285	=	£226	+	£59
C	£52,000	=	£31,400	+	£20,600
D	£4,900	=	£3,400	+	£1,500

Now lets look at the format of the BS. The simple layout is:

	Assets	Liabilities
Fixed	———————	—————
Current	———————	—————
	=	

You can re-work the statement so that all the assets, less the current liabilities, will equal the capital and other long-term liabilities. This is the basis for the standard statement that we normally see today.

Standard Balance Sheet layout

	Cost	Less depreciation	= Net Value
Fixed assets			
Current assets	_____		
Less current liabilities			_____
= <u>Working capital</u>			=========
= <u>Net assets</u>			_____
Financed by			=========
(Long-term liabilities)			

Note that the total of the Financed by section always BALANCES (equals) with the total net assets. We will cover depreciation in the next section. The working capital figure that you see (which is current assets less current liabilities) shows the amount of money available to run the business on a day-to-day basis. You'll see why this is important when we look at cash and stocks in Chapter 7.

Here's a balance sheet to practise by using the following information and the standard layout as above:

	(£)	(£)
Cash and floats	1,700	
Amounts due to suppliers	4,300	
Amounts due from customers	500	
Profit for the year	1,200	
Equipment	22,000	
Food stocks	1,150	
Owners Capital	27,000	

Here's the answer:

		= <u>Net value</u>
Fixed assets		
Equipment		<u>22,000</u>
Current assets		
Debtors	7,650	

Stocks	1,150	
Cash	1,700	
Total	10,500	
Less current liabilities		
Creditors	(4,300)	
Total	(4,300)	
= Working capital		6,200
= Net assets		28,200
Financed by		
Profit		1,200
Capital for year		27,000
Total		28,200

TIP

What if it doesn't balance?

First, tick off all your entries (on the question and on your answer) again to check that they've all been used.

Second, check all your additions and subtractions. If these don't work, see what the difference is between the two figures. Can you see a figure on the BS that is the same? If so (and this isn't likely if you've done the first step) see if you've written it correctly.

If you are still out of balance then divide the difference by two. Can you find this new figure anywhere? If so, then you will have added it instead of subtracting, or vice versa – doing this *doubles* the variance.

Make the correction and then check the balance again.

If you still don't balance then it's likely you've done this adding/subtracting mistake more than once, so check everything again and you should find the error.

Owners' returns

Lastly owners will also look at the return on the capital they have invested. There are some very complex calculations you can use which are based on company reports (see Chapter 10) but you can also do a simple calculation which compares the profit to the capital as a percentage. The formula is:

$$\text{Return on investment} = \frac{\text{Profit}}{\text{Capital invested}} \%$$

Adjustments to Accounts

Cost of Sales

First, one you are probably familiar with. Most hospitality businesses have stocks of one sort or another and the value of this (particular if it's alcohol) can be very high. You don't want to show all this as sold the moment you've purchased it as this would distort your figures and accounts have to show the cost of the items used to make the sales. So you need to ensure that the value of the items you haven't sold (stock) is shown on the BS and not on the P&L.

First you need to physically count the stocks (see Chapter 7) and then the value is used for the closing stock figure on the BS. In order to calculate the cost of sales – the amount used by customers – you need to use this formula:

Opening stock (your closing stock at the end of last month becomes the opening for this month)

Plus purchases and delivery charges etc.

Equals total stock available

Less cost of staff meals (even if off the customer menu)

Less the value of the closing stock

Equals what you have used to serve customers (cost of sales).

An example:

	(£)
Opening stock (as at the start of the period)	10,000
plus purchases	65,000
=	75,000
minus cost of staff meals	(5,000)
minus closing stock	(12,000)
= Cost of sales	58,000

Here's one to try: Opening stock £490, purchases £11,060, closing stock £530 and staff meals £920

The answer:

	(£)
Opening stock	490
plus purchases	11,060

=	11,550
minus cost of staff meals	(920)
minus closing stock	(530)
= Cost of sales	10,100

▶▶ ACTIVITY

Do you have CoS? Who calculates it? Are there any other additions or subtractions that have to be made before it can be finalized?

Prepayments

Some items have to be purchased in advance – for instance: annual rental or maintenance contracts. Here you don't want the whole amount to 'hit' your P&L all at one time as this will distort your profits. Instead they are *amortized* or split out for the months they refer to. It's classed as a current asset because technically we own it as it's been paid for.

	(£)
Contract (per year)	24,000
Charge per month	2,000
End April 2 months used	4,000
10 months outstanding (prepayment)	20,000

The prepaid amount stays on the BS, reducing each month when the charge goes to the P&L.

Try this:

Rental on equipment per year £10,400. How much is the prepayment per period if there are 13 periods per year?

If the invoice is paid in January (the first period of the financial year) and now is the eighth period, how much has been amortized (used) and how much remains on the BS?

Answer:

	(£)
Rental per year	10,400
Per 4 weekly period is (divide by 13)	800
Eight periods amortised to the P&L	6,400
Five periods remaining on the BS	4,000

Accruals

For the current liabilities an Accrual is the opposite of a prepayment – it's something that has been used but not yet paid for. At the end of each month it's unlikely that you will have been billed for everything so there tends to be a few days worth or, for instance, electricity, that has been used but not charged for. You may also have not been billed for food or drink delivered on the last day of the month. It's a current liability because it's owed to suppliers although hasn't yet been invoiced (creditors are those that have invoiced you and are ready to be paid).

	(£)
Electricity bill to 12 September (28 days worth)	560
Approximate daily usage	20
Accrue 18 days	360

There would be a charge to the electricity code on the P&L as a cost and to the accruals on the BS.

▶▶ **ACTIVITY**

Can you think of any more examples of items needing to be accrued in your area?

Depreciation

The most complex month-end adjustment is usually for depreciation. First we need to look at the Fixed Assets category again. You'll have seen that these are items that are likely to last more than a year and are high in original cost. Again it would be too expensive for them to be charged totally to the P&L when bought (though different companies have different rules on this).

You need to estimate how long they will last before they need replacement, and charge out a proportion of the cost each month. The main method is called 'straight line' and assumes that the items lose value at the same pace each month and year. Figure 2.4 shows what the value would look like.

Item costing £5,000 depreciated over 5 years so the value divided into 5 equal parts				
£1,000	£1,000	£1,000	£1,000	£1,000
Year 1	Year 2	Year 3	Year 4	Year 5

Figure 2.4 Straight line depreciation

Hence the same amount is charged out each year, divided equally per month. Here's an example: Cost £12,000, estimated lifespan is 5 years (normally expressed as 20%) so the depreciation is £200 per month or £2,400 a year.

	(£)
Purchase	12,000
Depreciation Year 1	(2,400)
Balance at end Year 1	9,600
Depreciation Year 2	(2,400)
Balance at end Year 2	7,200
Depreciation Year 3	(2,400)
Balance at end Year 3	4,800
Depreciation Year 4	(2,400)
Balance at end Year 4	2,400
Depreciation Year 5	(2,400)
Balance at end Year 5	0

The charge is subtracted from the Fixed Assets on the BS and then appears as a Fixed Charge on the bottom of the P&L, after the GOP line as it isn't controllable.

Reducing balance and valuation are two other methods that are not used very much now so we won't bother with them.

Here's a depreciation calculation for you to do:

Equipment £6,800 depreciated at 10% per annum (= 10 years' life)

Furniture £2,600, depreciated at 20% per annum (= 5 years' life)

Item	Cost (£)	Rate (%)	Amount (£)	Net (at end year 1) (£)
Equipment	6,800 10		680	6,120
Furniture	2,600 20		520	2,080

Now let's try and do everything so far. This exercise needs you to calculate depreciation and so on, prepare a P&L and then the BS. Note that the Net profit from the P&L goes to the BS and is added to last year's profit to date to give a cumulative profit. You could also calculate some percentages.

TIP

Do the workings out first – for prepayments, accruals, cost of sales and depreciation. This makes it easier to put together the P&L and BS.

Rural restaurant

The accounts list the following balances for the year ending December. You are asked to prepare the P&L and Balance Sheet.

	£		£
Floats	40	Repairs and maintenance	850
Drawings	2,000	Equipment	6,800
Sales	26,568	Furniture	2,600
Creditors	1,680	Payroll	5,890
Owners capital	22,340	Stock as at previous year	492
Rates	580	China, glass & silver	1,000
Utilities	930	Laundry	826
Marketing	200	Miscellaneous expenses	2,352
Purchases	10,988	Debtors	1,040
Buildings	12,000	Cash at bank	2,000

The following transactions have not yet been processed.

Stock at the end of this year	536	Accrual for utilities unpaid	228
Prepayment on rates	116	Accrual for wages unpaid	60
Marketing prepaid	40	Staff meals	920

No depreciation has been made. Depreciate equipment at 10% p.a.; furniture at 15% p.a.

Answer:

Workings out

Depreciation	Rate	Value	Depreciation
	(%)	(£)	(£)
Equipment	10	6,800	680
Furniture	15	2,600	390
		9,400	1,070

Prepayment	Value	Prepay	Net
	(£)	(£)	(£)
Rates	580	116	464
Marketing	200	40	160
		156	624

Accrual	Value	Accrue	Net
Utilities	930	228	1,158
Payroll	5,890	60	5,950
		288	7,108

Cost of sales calculation

	£	(%)
Opening stock	492	
Plus purchases	10,988	
Less staff meals	(920)	

	(%)	(£)	(£)
Less closing stock		(536)	
Equals CoS		10,024	

Profit & Loss Report

	(£)	(£)
Sales	26,568	100.0
Less cost of sales	(10,024)	(37.7)
Gross profit	16,544	62.3
Less payroll	(5,950)	(22.4)
	10,594	39.9
Less other expenses		
Utilities	(1,158)	(4.4)
Marketing	(160)	(0.6)
Repairs & maintenance	(850)	(3.2)
Staff meals	(920)	(3.5)
Laundry	(826)	(3.1)
Miscellaneous	(2,352)	(8.9)
Total	(6,266)	(23.6)
Gross operating profit	4,328	16.3
Less fixed charges		
Depreciation	(1,070)	(4.0)
Rates	(464)	(1.7)
	(1,534)	(5.8)
Net profit	2,794	10.5

Balance Sheet

Fixed Assets	Gross (£)	Depreciation (£)	Net (£)
Buildings	12,000		12,000
Equipment	6,800	(680)	6,120
Furniture	2,600	(390)	2,210
China, glass & silver	1,000		1,000
			21,330

Current Assets	
Cash	2,000
Floats	40
Stocks	536
Prepayments	156
Debtors	1,040
	3,772

Current Liabilities	
Creditors	1,680
Accruals	288
	1,968

Working capital	<u>1,804</u>
Net assets	<u>23,134</u>
Financed by	
Capital	22,340
Plus profit	2,794
Less drawings	<u>(2,000)</u>
	<u>23,134</u>

Summary

In this chapter we've looked at the two principal reports that are used to help in the management of the hospitality business – the profit and loss and balance sheet reports. We have also reviewed the various activities and adjustments that need to take place in order for the month-end accounts to be assembled in order to present a 'true and fair view' of the business. You have:

▷ Reviewed the structure of the P&L report including the standard format known as the Uniform System

▷ Considered the basic principles pertaining to the balance sheet and reviewed the layout in current common usage

▷ Practised calculating accruals, prepayments and depreciation

▷ Learned of the need for a format that shows 'common size' to allow comparisons

▷ Practised some common ratios.

Quiz

1. What goes in fixed assets?

2. What are current liabilities?

3. If your electricity bill is charged until 25th July, what happens to the 26-31st consumption?

4. If you had an oven costing £6,000 and estimated it would last 10 years, how much depreciation do you charge per year?

5. What does GOP stand for?

6. What's the best way to find the true cost of sales?

3

Managing revenue

▼
▼
▼
▼
▼

Features of different sectors ◀

Identifying areas for action ◀

Improving revenues ◀

Improving sales ◀

Introduction

Maximizing revenues is an important as minimizing costs to achieve profits. The usual (sales and marketing) approach is to try and gain additional business – and we will cover some of this here. However, since this is a book about control we'll be looking more at ways of ensuring that you get all your revenue from existing customers.

If you work in a section where only costs occur, much of this chapter may seem irrelevant, but you may have 'revenue' from a subsidy or allowance and you certainly still have customers. I hope you will gain an insight into practices in other sectors that may help you in the future, if not just now.

You have to ensure that everything a customer consumes is actually paid for and that you aren't giving it away, wasting it or losing it to fraud. This applies to a take-away meal, a drink, a package holiday or a five-star meal – all can lose revenues by inadequate control. In some sectors this may be more obvious as they have much stronger control mechanisms – in others it may be difficult to see easily where problems might occur.

We look at pricing in Chapter 5 but it's important to recognize now that there shouldn't be a conflict between marketing and control – the stakeholder approach means that everybody is interested in the business doing well. The controller wants good revenues as well as the marketing manager because this should result in good profits, which means good employment for them (in all its aspects).

By the end of this chapter you should be able to:

▷   Identify the features which may impact on revenue maximization

▷   Identify where shortfalls can occur, using ratios

▷   Calculate ratios for a range of revenue areas

▷   Find methods of improving revenues.

Features of different sectors

Before we look at some general areas of controlling revenue let's look at some more features of the hospitality industry that might influence revenue patterns and hence control processes. Many of these features are common to several hospitality sectors, to a greater or smaller extent.

Nature of the product

The product may be very complex (leisure hotels, cruise lines, theme parks) or very simple. A guesthouse may offer room and breakfast only, with no restaurant, room service, bar or other facilities. A fish-and-chip shop may sell only eight or 10 items, being more interested in concentrating on speed of service than the range of products.

One single purchase may have several elements – a take-away order could include a dozen things and so can a package holiday. All these elements can be different in behaviour and so need controlling in different ways.

Even within a single identifiable product you may have lots of different prices available – a business class hotel may sell a standard single room at 10 different rates to separate types of customer, from the quoted 'rack rate' to a heavily discounted one for a favoured client. A double measure of gin may be priced differently if sold during a 'happy hour', in a cocktail or as a standard product – and differently again if in a mini-bar. Airline or rail tickets can be discounted at different rates depending on how far in advance you buy them. Pricing at different levels is covered in Chapter 5.

Seasonality

Some businesses and sectors have distinct peaks and troughs in trade and 'seasonality' causes natural rises and falls independent of one-off economic changes. Seasonality is mainly used to mean different times of the year but you also get changes from day to day, such as

▷   The 'banquet season' before Christmas when the majority of balls and dinner dances are held

▷   Resorts may be strongly dependent on the weather

▷   Attractions are noticeably busier in school holidays and at weekends

▷   Soup bars and hot food counters may be far busier in cold wet weather than on warm summer days.

Mixed markets

Some sectors have very strongly defined markets whereas others such as fast food appeal to a much wider range of customers. Contract caterers may offer different types of meal to the same group of employees – a main caféteria, a deli-bar and hospitality suites. Individual guests may change their market type – for instance they will spend a lot of money on a meal if on company business (say £80 per person if they're not paying!) but if they take their family for a meal (with their own money) then a spend of £10-15 each is more likely.

One business may have one type of market at one time and a different type at another. Restaurants offer fixed-price menus at lunchtime to attract office workers but in the evening have an a-la-carte menu to attract a different type of customer who will stay a lot longer and spend more money. Levels of trade in pubs vary dramatically with the time of day and day of the week. Another example would be a leisure club that takes groups of schoolchildren during weekdays but individuals in the evenings and at weekends.

All these form *market segments*, a term usually used in hotels to describe the different types of customers. Here you may get 'rack rate' (full rate) guests, business grade, tour groups, leisure, conference, airline crew and so on – a big hotel may have 17 different segments during a week.

A hospital may have patients, visitors and staff and a university have residential and commercial customers, students and staff. The occupancy statistics will include the split into segments as well as the overall result. Theme parks can split into age groups according to ticket type so that they can target their advertising to the right groups at the right time.

►► ACTIVITY

It's always useful to be able to identify where your customers come from. This helps you target your marketing differently to suit the different needs. Think about the customers where you work. Can you split them into 'market segments'?

Captive markets

These occur for such customers as factory workers or hospital staff (as well as patients, army employees or prisoners) and may seem to automatically generate revenue but there's a real danger that the customers can easily get 'menu fatigue'. This has the effect that they might start to bring their own sandwiches, or sneak out to the pub at lunchtime, so there's an employment as well as feeding issue here.

Competition

Another issue can be competition for supply. A 'competitor analysis' is normally used to find the direct competition for your business (other restaurants, pubs and so on) but you could also use it on a smaller scale to see if there is any other type of competition. For a pub this could be not just other pubs and wine bars but people going to the off-licence and taking beer home for a 'night in'. Supermarkets are competition for restaurants now with their ranges of ready meals and you can rent a video (to go with those beers) instead of going to the cinema.

Another example seen recently has been the impact of mobile telephones on hotel telephone revenues. Phoning from a guest room has traditionally been quite expensive (the hotel has to cover the cost of its switchboard, the operator and so on) so guests now tend to use their own mobiles with a consequent loss of revenue to the hotel.

▶▶ **ACTIVITY**

Think about how a supermarket sells its products to different target markets. Loyalty schemes aren't just to persuade you to buy by giving you points – they are also designed to find out lots about your spending patterns and target you 'individually' as a customer.

Identifying areas for action

There are two main ways of identifying areas that you need to address — Ratios and Management By Walking About (MBWA).

MBWA

Nothing can beat the effectiveness of an alert manager's eye, both for seeing problems (and hopefully good things too) and for ensuring that correct actions are taken. If a manager or supervisor is seen to be watching what happens and reacts to it then the staff will also be alert. Taking action means praising the good things and highlighting those that need improvement. If there is a problem then you can discuss changing the approach, retrain staff or add new checks as needed. By 'leading from the top' your staff will strive harder for perfection too.

Some people steal or are wasteful if they have the opportunity, and watching what they are doing reduces this. If you show that you don't approve of it, they are less likely to steal as well. By maintaining staff morale and ensuring that they are treated fairly you will improve attitudes to control. You may not be able to influence pay levels (poor pay is another reason for theft) but you can reward staff in other ways (praise, nomination for Employee of the Month, telling senior management, and so on). Showing you care matters in more ways than one.

Mini-case

A member of staff suddenly started making mistakes with a consequent loss in his bar takings. He'd always been an excellent employee but now there were clear grounds for disciplinary action. The manager noticed that the barman looked haggard and unwell. It emerged that he and his family had been mugged in their own home the previous week and as a result he couldn't sleep well. They gave him some time off and two weeks later he returned, back to his old efficient self again.

Using ratios

We looked at the general reasons for using ratios in the previous Chapter. You as a manager or supervisor can't see everything. Using ratios can identify areas for concern so you can then target your actions. If you work in a hotel front office area you won't be able to work 24 hours a day (well, not every day!) and the night staff check in guests too. By using occupancy and housekeeping reports you can make sure that all rooms occupied have been charged for. If the average spend achieved per customer falls (in any type of unit) then you know you've got a problem with customers either not being charged for everything or staff pocketing the takings. You can identify both control problems and opportunities for increasing revenues through marketing and selling.

Performance for revenue areas is measured by:

▷   Variance analysis – comparing actual to budget, as we did in Chapter 2

▷   Daily, weekly and monthly sales

▷   Occupancy

▷   Average spend per customer, by different types

▷   Sales mix

▷   Profitability percentages.

Here are some of the key ratios that are used in the business to show how effective management is at controlling revenue. The formula for calculating them is shown and then a brief explanation of how they are used. There appear to be a lot of them but they can really be divided into just a few types – those that look at the number of customers, those that look at how much they spend and then the comparisons between revenue types.

Once you have learned one type of ratio you can use it for different sectors – so although you will see occupancy ratios separately for F&B and rooms they are really very similar both in calculation and in meaning.

Volume

Let's review the ratios that look at volumes first – often known as 'occupancy'. These take the number of customers you achieve divided by the capacity. In hotels the capacity is rooms available, in restaurants this is seats available and in exhibition centres it's space for stands.

$$\text{Room occupancy \%} \quad = \quad \frac{\text{Rooms sold}}{\text{Rooms available}} \text{ \%}$$

This ratio looks at rooms sold as a proportion of rooms available. It gives you a measure of how efficient you are at selling the space you had available on the day. You could also use it for cabins sold on cruise ships or for long-stay hostels or apartments. You would normally do this calculation once per day and then for the month and the year. It's unlikely that you would achieve over 100% occupancy in a day unless you have a lot of day-lets (say to airline crews) and very efficient housekeeping staff.

Your customers may also be split into market segments – yes, you can split by segment and type although this is only worthwhile if your volumes are high enough. So there's no point in splitting too much if you only have 100 customers a day, but if you have 1,000 or 10,000 then it's definitely helpful.

TIP

Remember decimal points on percentages – always show at least one, e.g. 50.3% not 50%.

$$\text{Double occupancy} = \frac{\text{Double rooms sold}}{\text{Total rooms sold}} \%$$

Some accommodation sectors also look at the number of beds occupied. You can calculate this either by doing the bed occupancy (beds sold divided by beds available) or by finding the number of double rooms sold as a proportion of the total. This result may be a bit distorted if you then have triple rooms or quadruples.

$$\text{Seat turnover} = \frac{\text{Covers sold}}{\text{Seats available}} \%$$

The same type of ratio can be used in food and beverage outlets. This uses the number of customers ('covers') divided by the seats you have available. For a small restaurant with a single sitting this may be less than 100% (a full house may be unusual) but for a staff caféteria each seat may be occupied several times in a day, so an occupancy of several hundred percent is usual. Sometimes this may be expressed as the number of times a seat is 'turned'.

$$\text{Average customers per day} = \frac{\text{Total customers per month}}{\text{Number of days in period/month}}$$

$$\text{Customers per hour} = \frac{\text{Total customers}}{\text{Number of hours in day}}$$

$$\text{Passengers per flight} = \frac{\text{Total passengers}}{\text{Number of flights}}$$

$$\text{Visitors per day} = \frac{\text{Total visitors}}{\text{Number of days in period/month}}$$

$$\text{Average covers per meal period} = \frac{\text{Covers sold}}{\text{Number of meals in period}}$$
(can be done for separate meals – breakfast, lunch, dinner)

All these are really the same sort of ratio – they show the average volume of customers over a period. This is useful as an overall guide and for comparing to budget or to last year but for use in planning (see the chapter on forecasting) you really need to plot these on a daily or an hourly basis to see the peaks and troughs in the business. Casinos use two similar ratios –

Average Time Played (at a table or on a slot machine) and 'Decisions Per Hour' which means the number of bets that are made for the time that they play.

Spends per customer

Now let's look at how much they spend. We'll mainly look at revenue but also consider profit. You'll notice that the results are given in pounds and pence – as mentioned in Chapter 2, this is always done with ratios.

Average room rate
(hotels, hostels, residential, cruises)
$$= \frac{\text{Rooms revenue}}{\text{Rooms sold}} \; £p$$

Spend per customer
(Cover, café guest, hospital visitor, traveller, attraction visitor, shop purchaser and so on)
$$= \frac{\text{Revenue}}{\text{Customers}} \; £p$$

Average Bet *(casino)*
$$= \frac{\text{Total betting revenue}}{\text{Customers}} \; £p$$

The total revenue is divided it by the number of customers – whatever they are called (guests, patients, covers and so on). You can do this for overall revenue for the period but it has more value if split into different categories such as food, beverage, retail, entrance fees, beauty therapy – the list is endless. This really helps you see where the sales are coming from, and can then be matched with costs (see next chapter). You can identify which areas are more popular with others, and then consider re-vitalizing those that are performing badly.

As with occupancy, you can also split revenue into the market segments to give average spend for different types of customer and into trading periods.

TIP

Remember decimal points again – for money amounts per person always show the pounds and pennies, e.g. £10.16 not £10.

You can also consider the revenue generated by the space you have available:

Room hire per square metre
(by day or month)
$$= \frac{\text{Room hire revenue}}{\text{Number of square metres of space}} \; £p$$

Retail revenue per square metre
(by day or month)
$$= \frac{\text{Retail revenue}}{\text{Number of square metres of retail space}} \; £p$$

A further ratio that is used in hotels is yield, which is a measure of efficiency of both average occupancy and average room rate. You first need to calculate revenue per available room (REVPAR) – the average revenue gained from all the rooms you had available (not those actually sold). This is shown in pounds and pence and is used extensively to compare one hotel against another, published in comparisons of operating statistics (see the reading list).

The yield ratio takes the REVPAR figure and compares it to the optimum average rate – usually the 'rack' (or published) rate – as a percentage. This shows you how efficient you are in selling both rate and rooms.

REVPAR – Revenue per available room
(per day)

$$= \frac{\text{Rooms Revenue}}{\text{Rooms Available}} \quad £p$$

Yield

$$= \frac{\text{Revpar}}{\text{Potential average room rate}} \quad \%$$

Profit ratios

The final ratios in this section are to do with profits and you can calculate these for any type of customer as well as show them as a percentage.

Profit per customer

$$= \frac{\text{Net profit}}{\text{Number of Customers}} \quad £p$$

Profit per Staff Member
(you could also calculate sales per staff member, especially if they earn bonuses or commission based on sales)

$$= \frac{\text{Net profit}}{\text{Number of Staff}} \quad £p$$

Net Profit %

$$= \frac{\text{Net Profit}}{\text{Sales}} \quad \%$$

Here's an example for you to do:

		Occupancy(%)
Rooms available	90	
Rooms sold		
Rack rate	10	
Tour group	5	
Business	60	
TOTAL		

Rooms revenue	Total	Average room rate
Rack rate	£350	
Tour group	£325	
Business	£3,300	
TOTAL		

TIP

The overall average room rate isn't the average of the three room rates – it's the total rooms revenue divided by the total rooms sold. Try both ways if you wish and see the difference.

Here's the answer:

Rooms Revenue	(£)	Average room rate (£)
Rack rate	350	35.00
Tour group	325	65.00
Business	3,300	55.00
TOTAL	3,975	53.00
Occupancy		
Rooms sold		Occupancy (%)
Rack rate	10	11.1
Tour group	5	5.6
Business	60	66.7
	75	83.3

Sales mix

Finally you can look at the proportion of individual sales to total sales, and express it as a percentage. The usual split is by type of revenue (food and beverage, retail and entrance fees, for instance) but you can also split by meal or trading period. This shows you how much money is being taken at particular times of day or from different sources and again is really useful when it comes to planning for the future. This split will affect the costs too.

$$\text{Food} = \frac{\text{Food sales}}{\text{Total F\&B sales}} \%$$

$$\text{Retail sales} = \frac{\text{Retail sales}}{\text{Total sales}} \%$$

$$\text{Breakfast sales} = \frac{\text{Breakfast sales}}{\text{Total café sales}} \%$$

▶▶ ACTIVITY

Can you think of any more ratios? Consider your area (or one that you know) and see what type of revenue ratios are calculated. Are there any more that could be done but aren't?

Here's a very simple example:

	(£)	(%)
Room sales	14,000	70.0
Food sales	4,000	20.0
Beverage sales	2,000	10.0
Total sales	20,000	100.0

Improving revenues generally

Now let's review ways of improving revenues. Some are marketing ideas but others are more to do with control – and both are considered in terms of improving efficiency without increasing workload (too much).

Improving controls

Some areas of revenue have few problems in collecting revenue – no money equals no ticket, for instance. Effective systems (physical, administrative and technological) are crucial in helping maximise revenues (and in minimizing costs, of course). Once installed then you should be able to limit your audit processes to spot-checking where necessary, without having to cross-check every transaction.

Till systems

In brief, manual tills are cheap but time-consuming whereas electronic systems are simple to operate and allow staff to concentrate on serving the customer, but expensive to purchase initially (though you can rent them instead).

Electronic point of sale systems (EPOS) range from quite simple to very sophisticated mini computers – the more you spend, the more control and information you get. The essentials are keys with pre-set prices (so staff can't charge differently), the calculation of change for customers and end-of-day reports which summarize sales and cash. More sophisticated systems will give you a full menu-mix analysis which tells you not only how many you have sold but the cost and selling price of every item. This is really useful as you can see the revenue that you should have taken for the items that have been sold, and can take action if the figures don't match.

EPOS systems can be linked to a central computer that will monitor peaks and troughs throughout the day (so enabling you to keep track of supplies and staffing) and can have the prices instantly updated. Some can also manage loyalty schemes for you by collating 'points' earned by your customers which can then be exchanged for free or discounted drinks or meals.

You may even have seen 'hand-held' EPOS systems in use. Waiting staff use terminals to take orders that are then transmitted directly to the kitchen (and the customer's bill) without the waiting staff having to leave the customer. This can improve service speed enormously (especially if the kitchen and restaurant are a long way apart) and certainly gives the impression of attentive service. Another sector that has started to use hand-helds is on-train catering where the amount of space available for the buffet-car (or trolley) staff is very limited. These will also print receipts if the customer needs one but can be a little slow to operate (a nuisance when you've 20 commuters in a queue all needing a cup of coffee).

Property-wide systems

Property management systems (PMS) are much more sophisticated computerized systems that run a whole series of functions, usually in a hotel. In the past these were limited to front-office operations but are now usually integrated both into yield management systems and into the main back office accounting system – some computers run all three together in one integrated, designed framework. This means that the entire hotel can route all business through one system. Figure 3.1 shows the flow of information goes like this:

Figure 3.1 Flow chart for Property management system

Losses also occur from either under-ringing or incorrect pricing, so it's crucial to ensure that your billing system is up to date and that there are controls in place to stop errors. If you don't have an EPOS or PMS then you need to ensure that all items consumed are paid for. This means meals, drinks, rooms, rides, beauty treatments and rounds of golf.

Control systems for different sectors

Restaurants

The usual system in restaurants and cafés is to write a guest check in duplicate for the food and one copy is exchanged for the food when cooked. The other copy goes to the cashier (if there is one) for the guest bill. These guest checks are numbered so they can be tracked and not re-used. You need to then make sure that the bill is paid, of which more in Chapter 7. If you are using a manual system then it's important to spot-check all these guest checks to see whether every order was served and paid for and that all have been used for what was intended.

For self-service restaurants you either need to have a till at the end of the counter or to be very vigilant to ensure that customers don't walk in – and then eat and walk out without paying. Breakfast in hotels can be a particular issue if you don't check off all room numbers as guests enter the restaurant. The location of the tills does help with maximization collection of revenue and so, in a food court where there are lots of counters (and hence it looks like a buffet) the tills should be situated so customers are funnelled through them to the seating areas.

Mini-case

A family were staying in a hotel and invited friends to dinner. The restaurant operated a Carvery-style operation whereby guests ordered their starter and then chose their own main course. The restaurant manager took their order, noted their room number and that there were two extra covers to be charged. When they checked out at the end of their stay they found that the two extra had not been charged for – a potential loss of £31.

Pubs and bars

In bars and pubs the routine is normally for the customer to order and then give cash in exchange for the drink – which in theory maximises revenue immediately. EPOS systems help ensure customers are charged the correct prices so that there is less opportunity for staff to overcharge and pocket the excess. Drinking is part of the culture and any drinks for staff must correctly accounted for, whether paid for by customers or by the establishment.

There is the ability now to pay for drinks by credit card, providing that an on-going record is kept so that the customer pays for all the correct items consumed. It's often worth having the guest sign for each round separately – if they have too many then they may be incapable of signing the check by the time the bill is presented.

Subsidized and full-cost catering

The subsidy (whether part or total) is often based on the number of customers you serve whether for hospital patients, employee feeding or army trainees. In order to achieve the maximum subsidy you need to ensure that all your customers are counted, and that your number served matches with the figure produced by the organization paying for it.

This might mean a cross-check between patients registered for treatment and number of lunches served, or staff signing for meals with time-clock records. Again there's an element of trust but this time between contractor and contractee, so it's important that you maintain that by being as accurate as possible. Even if you have been paid in advance for these customers you still need to ensure that your records are accurate so that you can ensure your cost percentages (see next chapter) are kept in line.

Conference and banqueting and event catering

These operate with very high numbers and often a tight turn-round on meal times, so ensuring that you have recorded all the guests is crucial. The process starts early. Contracts (such as a Banquet Event Order) must be signed off by the organizer for groups, banquets, conferences and so on so that there are no disputes later. This type of agreement means there should be no confusion for anybody, from the head of the company holding the function to the banqueting porter who has to move all the tables around. Again, it's about maximizing revenue by minimizing potential problems.

Once the guests actually sit down to eat you can check the number against those booked and the meals delivered from the kitchen. This can be almost impossible with a stand-up buffet!

Complimentary meals

Complimentary can mean a meal given as compensation for bad service (hopefully rare) or for a different business reason such as delays in check-in at a hotel or airport. In catering managers and staff may seem to be eating 'comps' as part of training – tasting a new menu, for instance. A major part of the food and accommodation offered in casinos may be 'comped' in order to encourage punters to spend more money at the tables or on the machines.

Different companies have different attitudes to 'comps' – some account for it all at cost (and adjust the cost of sales figure), others record all at revenue which then shows the true number of customers served. What you need to ensure is that these are properly recorded and justified.

Rooms controls

Staff taking reservations need to ensure that all data is correct including billing and rates to be charged. Rooms-sold data is checked against house-keeping reports to ensure that all rooms occupied have been accounted for (paid for or for staff use). The difficulty is in ensuring that the rates charged are not discounted for friends or in return for personal reward. Chance guests, particularly late at night, may offer cash to pay for their room on check-in and it can be tempting for staff to pocket the cash rather than pay it in. Hence the need to cross-check the rooms occupied with the house-keeping report the next morning.

If you want to read more about rooms management and maximizing rooms revenue by yield management then please see the reading list.

Mini-case

A family booked a specific room at a hotel. When they checked in, they were allocated to a different room that was much smaller and had fewer facilities, although at a lower room rate (£97). They complained and the receptionist moved them to the room they had originally booked.

On check out they found they had only been charged the £97 rate – a potential loss to the hotel of £90 over the three nights. The receptionist had not changed the rate when they moved to the correct room. Yes – it was the same family who had the carvery meal, on the same stay – and they'd been undercharged on previous visits too.

What does this say about the management's (and company's) attitude to control?

Comps are relevant for rooms too. The courier of a tour group is also normally comped so this needs to be carefully costed into the package price you are offering – it isn't really 'free'. Again different companies use different approaches. Usually the cost of the meal or accommodation has already been budgeted for against a cost code and so is charged there – these shouldn't be set against revenue or it will give an inaccurate picture of volumes and spends.

Mini-case

An international hotel group had recently opened its first hotel in London. It seemed like the entire senior management of the company decided it was essential to pay a site visit – and asked for complimentary accommodation. The GM complained that this was affecting his revenue, as he couldn't sell to 'paying punters'. Head office agreed and insisted that everybody paid full ('rack') rate so that occupancy and average spend were maintained and the figures not distorted.

Surprisingly, once they were asked to pay, demand from these senior personnel declined!

Improving sales

Now more about marketing and upselling. Here are a range of ideas that are found in most marketing books, so apologies if you've seen them all before. There are a few comments added about the financial implications – which *aren't* always mentioned by marketers.

You can either improve sales by selling more to your existing customers, or increase the number of customers overall. First you need to use ratios to see where the opportunities are – there's no point in trying to increase customers if you don't have the capacity, enough staff or the right equipment.

Increasing spends

Training and incentives

Trained staff are crucial in explaining dishes (or other products for sale), persuading customers to buy (upselling), serving correct portions, collecting payment and generally keeping customers happy – whatever the type of operation. Happy customers spend more (and tip better)!

Incentive schemes for staff can be very good in persuading them to upsell to customers, and can help in staff morale, which is likely to mean fewer problems with theft and wastage. Awareness of the impacts on profits helps staff identify where to focus their energies – it's better to promote items with a higher GP – so try and sell a pot of tea rather than an orange juice. It is called *menu engineering* and is a technique for persuading people to eat different things that will generate more profit, or perhaps are easier to process (and hence less resource-intensive).

Yield or revenue management

This is an approach used in hotels (and airlines, sports stadia and for car hire) that boosts both rate and occupancy. You can read up about this in other books if you want to (see reading list) but the basic approach is to try to persuade people to stay at the times that you are quieter. If they want to stay at a premium period then a premium price is charged, such as for package holidays during school holiday periods. Off-peak prices on trains are infinitely cheaper than peak prices to encourage people to travel more. An example for a ticket to London:

07.00 Commuters   Price £38
08.00 Late commuters, some leisure travellers   Price £18
09.00 Leisure travellers, with discount card   Price £12

So by travelling two hours later you can save two-thirds of the price – for the same type of seat on the same type of train, for the same journey.

Diversification of sale items

This means adding more items for sale that customers will buy as extras to their main product. If you have a teashop you could add a few postcards, pots of jam or craft items – they would look attractive on display (saving the cost of display china, for instance) and could give you extra revenue. A sandwich bar can sell coffee as well as soft drinks and a package holiday offer optional city tours. Some hotels or restaurants display original pictures by local artists on their walls – these save on the cost of buying your own, support local enterprise and can give you commission on every one sold.

You do need to make sure the revenue is kept separate from your own, though, so that there is no dispute at a later stage, either with the supplier or the tax inspector.

►► ACTIVITY

Think of somewhere you visit as a customer (your local swimming pool would do). Do they have other products on sale? Could they diversify and offer additional products or service that would add value to your visit and revenue for themselves.

Now think if there is anything your own business could do to add revenue by adding new products or services.

Increasing customers

First of all you need to ensure that you have the capacity to cope with an increase (enough space, staff, equipment, materials and so on). You then need to forecast (see Chapter 6) where your peaks and troughs will be. At peak times you probably have enough business to cope with, but you should be able to identify troughs that you could try to fill.

►► ACTIVITY

Look at your customer flows (do you have an EPOS or PMS, or a spreadsheet, that can help you here?). Try and plot your peaks and troughs on a chart (see Chapter 9 for some suggestions about presenting this). Do these occur at particular times of day or certain days of the week? Talk to your boss about whether you can increase customers in the low periods. If not, why not?

Special 'events' and offers

Special events can be good at attracting additional customers and persuading them to stay longer and spend more. Themed days or evenings can maximise revenues and satisfy customers, and in contract catering are good at preventing menu fatigue and encouraging customers to 'eat in' rather than bring their own. Special offers have a similar effect but can be run over a longer period – for instance a discount on a specific beer can be sponsored by a brewery, encourage more drinking and so generate more revenues and profits.

Daily specials on a menu can increase customers but more often will offer variety to existing customers (avoiding 'menu fatigue' which can cause numbers of customers to decrease). They also allow the business to use cheaper ingredients or use up excess stocks such as bin-ends. Happy hours are another way of encouraging more customers who hopefully will then continue to drink at full price.

Other special offers are geared at quiet times of the year. The 'lunch for a fiver' promotions seen both nationally and locally have been good at generating restaurant business in winter. Customers often try a new venue and, if they like it, may well come back and spend ten times that on an evening meal in the future. This happens in all sectors in different ways – everybody has 'sales' of one type of another to encourage people to buy products or services.

Diversification of products

Here we mean offering different products to persuade them against going to a competitor. Offering alternatives to a captive audience can also help. Since many office workers often want to 'desk-dine' – eat a sandwich at their desk to save time – then many caterers have diversified their products by offering, say, a deli-bar, a sandwich shop, vending machines and perhaps a coffee shop in addition to the standard facilities. You do need to consider costs, though, if you are going to open satellite branches – sometimes they just aren't cost-effective.

Diversification of markets

Finding new markets can help improve revenues a lot, especially if your business is seasonal, as in a university town. Here local business must attract different types of customers, such as tourists, during holiday periods in order to maximise revenues in all aspects of hospitality – visitors will stay in hotels,

Mini-case

An airport terminal had a satellite departure area with a snack bar. Unfortunately only two flights a day used this gate, but the authorities insisted on keeping the snack bar open 'just in case' passengers happened to wander down there while waiting for a flight at another gate.

The caterer argued that this was creating a loss as it was far too expensive for them to operate like this and it had a negative effect on passengers as they saw tired food and depressed staff – but the authorities didn't see it that way.

The situation was only resolved when the airport increased its number of flights and had to use this satellite gate much more – with a consequent increase in sales for both caterer and airport authority.

eat in restaurants, drink in pubs, visit attractions, take tours and shop for souvenirs. Even schools are experimenting with opening for breakfast to increase sales and so cover more of the fixed costs (and there's an added bonus of ensuring the children are at school on time and aren't hungry).

Discounts

Offering a discount can be a short-term way of encouraging business. Supermarkets are very good at persuading us to buy things and we can learn a lot from their techniques. The 'buy-one-get-one-free' isn't just to sell soap powder – you'll go in and buy other things as well. A good hospitality example is a hotel offering 'Sunday night at half price if you stay Friday and Saturday' – Sundays may be traditionally quiet and hotel guests usually spend money in the restaurant and bar especially if they have had a 'good deal' on their room.

Pizza restaurants can do it too on quieter days, or at slow times of the day (say mid-afternoon). If you take advantage of the offer then you will usually buy a drink and perhaps a dessert (with high GPs), which will be charged at full price and make profits for the business. Airlines offer discounts at quieter times of year – it may seem a cheap flight but you could buy tobacco or perfume on board and if you like the airline return later for another, more expensive flight. The 'loss leader' approach works in hospitality too!

We'll look a bit more at how to ensure costs are still covered in the next two chapters.

Mini-case

A main-line rail station concourse was being redeveloped. The operators of the station thought that there were vast numbers of 'uncaptured' customers and that offering different products would expand the number of people buying food. In turn this might mean that they would spend money on other things too – all of which would mean more in the way of commission to themselves.

A supermarket was installed to the dismay of the existing outlets who saw the cheaper products available competing for their own business. These experienced operators immediately took action to change the type of product they sold so that they weren't competing – they had identified new potential markets who would buy premium sandwiches, soup and snacks. They were happy, the supermarket was happy and the station operators were happier still (all the way to the bank).

Help from outside

'Mystery shoppers' are hired by the company to check on all aspects of service and control. A mystery shopper poses as a guest and observes incognito (without being rumbled) before reporting back on all aspects of the guest service and control to ensure everything is operating to standard. There's a danger this can be used as a 'police officer' approach whereas it's better to consider this as another management tool that will highlight where things are going well, and where needs improvement. They are trained in the business so will suggest improvements as well as pointing out issues.

Customer feedback

This can be really beneficial in telling you what customers think about your products and services and what's working and what's not. There are several ways of finding out – questionnaires, face-to-face discussion, focus groups and so on. See some of the books on the reading list for more details.

▶▶ ACTIVITY

Next time you go out for a meal why not be a 'mystery shopper' yourself?
Do the staff try and optimize sales – sell you an extra bread roll or coffee after the meal, for instance? What about the marketing of the meal – does the menu entice you to eat? Does the ambience of the restaurant help you relax (or is it designed for high turnover so you're encouraged to eat up and get out as quickly as possible)? Would you return?
Is there anything you can learn from their sales and marketing techniques that will help you in your job? Are there any control issues you can spot – undercharging, for instance?

One more point. The 'quality experience' is intended to lead to a satisfied customer who will spend money, return at a future date, spend more money and then tell other people – it is normally far cheaper to keep an existing customer than to find a new one.

Excercise

Here's an exercise for you to do which will test a few of the skills covered in this (and the previous) Chapter. You can calculate variances and the percentage variance. You can then calculate the percentages to sales, and even the cost percentages – the same format applies. Lastly you can look at the other ratios and see if you can do those. Are there any more you could do?

BUT... what does this mean? Try and interpret the figures and identify where there are problems.

When you look at the answer you'll see some discussion about the variances and some ideas as to what may have happened.

Profit & Loss Report – Restaurant

28-day period	Budget	Budget (%)	Actual	Actual (%)	Variance	Variance (%)
Seats available	50		50			
Seats per period						
Covers sold	1,120		952			
Revenue						
Food	£20,100		£17,600			
Beverage	£6,700		£4,300			
Total						
Average spend /cover – food						
Average spend /cover – beverage						
Seat occupancy %						

And the answer:

Profit & Loss Report – Restaurant   28-day period

	Budget	Budget (%)	Actual	Actual (%)	Variance	Variance (%)
Seats available	50		50			
Seats per period	1,400	1,400	0	0.00		
Covers sold	1,120	952	(168)	(15.00)		
Revenue	(£)	(%)	(£)	(%)	(£)	(%)
Food	20,100	75.0	17,600	80.4	(2,500)	(12.44)
Beverage	6,700	25.0	4,300	19.6	(2,400)	(35.82)
Total	26,800	100.0	21,900	100.0	(4,900)	(18.28)
Average spend /cover – food (£)	17.95		18.49		0.54	3.0
Average spend /cover – beverage (£)	5.98		4.52		1.47	24.5
Seat occupancy (%)	80.00		68.00		12.00	15.0

So – what does it mean? Here are a few comments:

Customers — Seat occupancy is down by 15% – this means that, with an average of 34 seats occupied a day, 16 aren't sold. Can you identify why this is? Are any particular days worse than others are?

Average spend for food is up on budget, but beverage is down – so you should add the two together. This gives an overall actual of £23.01 whereas the budget was £23.93 – down almost 4%. Do you know why? Was the budget wrong (easy to say yes, with hindsight – but why did you set it as this)?

Together (occupancy and spend) means a shortfall of almost £5,000 on revenue – 18%. Is there anything happening locally that would affect both of these factors? If you can identify why things have gone wrong then perhaps you can do something about it.

Staff Dining Facilities

Here's another exercise for you to try, please fill in all the boxes. You will first find the totals and then calculate some revenue ratios. (Assume the facilities are closed each month for 8 weekend days, plus the bank holiday in August)

		July	August	September
	days in month			
		£	£	£
Sales	Deli-bar	12,800	10,000	15,250
	Food hall	26,500	22,500	39,500
Covers	Deli-bar	5,200	4,200	5,900
	Food hall	8,300	7,600	12,300
Average spends	Deli-bar			
	Food hall			
	Total			
Covers per day	Deli-bar			
	Food hall			
	Total			
Sales per day	Deli-bar			
	Food hall			
	Total			

Answer

		July	August	September
days in month		23	22	22
		£	£	£
Sales	Deli-bar	12,800	10,000	15,250
	Food hall	26,500	22,500	39,500
	Total	39,300	32,500	54,750
Covers	Deli-bar	5,200	4,200	5,900
	Food hall	8,300	7,600	12,300
Total		13,500	11,800	18,200
Average spends	Deli-bar	£2.46	£2.38	£2.58
	Food hall	£3.19	£2.96	£3.21
	Total	£2.91	£2.75	£3.01
Covers per day	Deli-bar	226	191	268
	Food hall	361	345	559
	Total	587	536	827
Sales per day	Deli-bar	£556.52	£454.55	£693.18
	Food hall	£1,152.17	£1,022.73	£1,795.45
	Total	£1,708.70	£1,477.27	£2,488.64

What can you work out from these numbers? What's the trend in customers and spends?

Summary

Within this third chapter we have focused on the revenue aspects of the hospitality business. Although some units or departments may not have sales there are still techniques here that may be helpful in the future. We have looked at both sales and control aspects and shown that the two cannot be treated independently – maximizing revenue relies on good management practice from both perspectives. Use of ratios allows comparisons between budget and actual so managers can identify where action needs to be taken. In this chapter you have, therefore:

▷ Identified a range of revenue areas for the different sectors

▷ Examined a range of ratios that can be used to analyse revenues

▷ Discussed techniques for improving revenue gained from customers

▷ Discussed a variety of techniques to increase the number of customers.

Quiz

1.   What is revenue?

2.   What are the two main ways of identifying problems?

3.   Can you identify the main ways of increasing revenue?

4.   How do you calculate occupancy?

5.   How do you calculate average spend?

4

Managing costs

▼
▼
▼
▼
▼

Types of cost ◀

Ratios ◀

Control of costs ◀

Raw materials ◀

Labour ◀

Other costs ◀

Introduction

In the previous chapter we discussed revenue and identified a range of areas where it can be improved by either sales or control techniques. However, in reality there may be only limited opportunities for you to improve revenues – or you may not have them at all. You then need to look at the other side of the P&L – costs. Controlling costs has always been more popular than controlling revenue with potentially large savings to be made by the manager, or so says the traditional view of the accountant.

In this chapter we'll look at the principles of controlling costs but within the constraints of maintaining the quality of customer service and product – which would result in an adverse effect on revenues. To do this we need to understand how costs behave, some being more controllable than others. You need to concentrate on managing what is manageable. As with revenue we'll also review the relevant ratios that will help indicate problems and then look at a range of techniques to minimize costs.

By the end of this chapter you will be able to:

▷   Identify the types of costs that occur in the various hospitality sectors

▷   Define cost behaviour and the difference between fixed and variable costs

▷   Calculate cost ratios

▷   Extract the fixed and variable elements from a series of total costs.

Types of costs

Many sectors rely on the effective control of costs in order to optimize the 'bottom line'. Managers can take simple actions which will have a significant effect on some of the costs, but other costs are relatively unmanageable. Hence, in order to target our attention and activities, we need to know how they behave – which are controllable, and which are not. First let's see the three main types of costs which are raw materials, labour and everything else (see Figure 4.1). We mentioned these in Chapter 2 when we looked at the P&L report. The 'everything else' can be split into departmental expenses, administrative expenses and property costs such as rent, rates and so on.

Figure 4.1 Types of costs

This type of classification doesn't really help us very much to manage costs because it doesn't tell you which you can control and which you can't (with the exception of the Fixed Charges below the GOP line, mentioned earlier). To really understand we need to re-classify costs into how they behave.

Costs can be *fixed*, *variable* or *semi-variable* (the terms 'mixed' or 'semi-fixed' are used in some textbooks).

Variable costs

Costs that are *variable* are totally dependent on the volume of sales. If you sell something then you incur a cost – so if you sell a bottle of cola you'll have the cost of that bottle. The main type of variable cost is the raw materials that make food and beverage (the cost of sales, in other words) but there are lots of other examples such as napkins, packaging for fast food, gift packs for guests, paper for printing tickets or guest bills. Some labour costs may be variable where you only employ staff if they have people to serve – banqueting is the most common example although takeaways try to operate on variable labour too.

These are relatively easy to manage as you shouldn't have a cost if there hasn't been a sale, but you do need to keep track of them to make sure things (such as bottles of cola) aren't going missing.

Fixed costs

Fixed costs, however, aren't affected by the volume of sales and so don't change much during the year. Typical examples are the fixed charges (rates, depreciation, and so on) already mentioned but there are also departmental and administrative costs which are stable, such as staff and management salaries, hire of equipment or flowers. It is difficult to manage these, as you must pay them no matter what the level of business in order to maintain quality.

Obviously if a staff member leaves then you can think about when or if you will recruit a replacement, but that's the only time you can really reduce this cost (you wouldn't like it if your boss suddenly decided not to pay you if there wasn't enough business, would you?).

Semi-variable costs

Some costs are a mixture of fixed and variable and are called *semi-variable* – and so some parts are controllable and other parts aren't. For example, if you have a guest house then you need to have the lights on all the time in the entrance hall (fixed) but a bedroom light is only on when the room is occupied (variable). Another common example is staff pay – their basic wage is fixed but any overtime worked is variable.

Figure 4.2 extends the diagram in Figure 4.1.

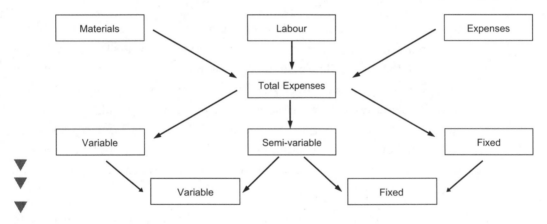

Figure 4.2 Types of costs

Other words you may hear quoted are 'direct' and 'indirect'. Direct costs are those able to be charged straight to a department. Indirect costs are generally those that belong to the property as a whole (including administration costs).

Different types of business

The disparate sectors all have these types but in varying proportions depending on how they operate and so different levels of controllability. In general, the higher priced the business is, the more likely they are to have greater fixed than variable costs. This is because they tend to have a higher number of permanent well-trained (fixed) staff and also standard expenses (flowers and music all the time, for instance). Lower priced sectors, such as takeaways, are more likely to have variable paper goods or labour (part-time and with limited skills).

It may also be the particular location that affects the cost behaviour. If you have a remote site (Hebridean island, oil rig, middle of the desert) you often have to transport almost everything in including the staff and all supplies. In these scenarios costs that might normally be variable can become semi-variable or fixed.

Ratios

As we did with revenue we can use ratios to identify where there are potential problems. These are mainly divided into two types – a cost per customer and a percentage. There are also productivity ratios related to how efficient your staff are in performing their jobs, although these aren't used in all sectors. We'll look at overall cost ratios first and then within each section look at specific ones that apply to that type of cost.

First we'll see the overall cost per customer ratios, which are exactly the same in concept as the revenue per customer ones we did in the last chapter – you take the amount and divide it by the number of people. Again the formula will be given followed by a short explanation.

Per customer costs

$$\text{Total cost per customer} \quad = \quad \frac{\text{Total Cost}}{\text{Number of customers}} \quad \text{£p}$$

This standard formula can be done per restaurant cover, fast food purchaser, theme park visitor, hotel guest, cruise ship passenger, staff eating in a catering facility – and so on. It's the total cost for any category on your P&L divided by the number of people served. The ratio is only appropriate (for control purposes) for those costs that are variable, so there's little point calculating the amount of depreciation cost per person, for instance.

As usual these can be compared to your budget (and to last year) and a variance calculated. This will show you how much you have deviated in cost per customer from what you planned. If the cost is fully variable then there shouldn't be a variance – and you need to investigate why this has happened. Once you've identified a reason, you should (hopefully) be able to take action.

Some sectors use these cost calculations as the most important ratio and monitor not just individual amounts but the total costs per customer. For airline catering, for instance, even a one-penny variation can mean a high cost or saving when multiplied by thousands of meals a day.

Cost versus quality

Remember that spending too little can be as bad as spending too much – yes the costs are reduced but what has happened to the customer product or service? Has there been a decrease in quality? Has the portion of chips been reduced, a staff member underpaid or overworked (or both) or the sheets not changed? All these affect the 'guest experience' and ultimately revenue. So – lower costs need investigating as much as higher ones do.

The one problem with average cost amounts is that they need to be taken in the context of the sales figure – if the average revenue per customer rises then often so will the average cost. To monitor this you need to look at percentages too.

Cost percentages

$$\text{Cost of Sales percentage (CoS\%)} \quad = \quad \frac{\text{Total cost of sales}}{\text{Sales}} \quad \%$$

$$\text{Gross Profit percentage (GP\%)} \quad = \quad \frac{\text{Gross profit}}{\text{Sales}} \quad \%$$

As you see, you can take the total cost of sales and express it as a percentage of the sales. These two have been shown together because they are two aspects of the same approach. The cost percentage takes the cost as a percentage of sales whereas GP% looks at the gross profit as a percentage of sales – it really depends on the business that they focus on. A low cost % = a high GP%, and vice versa. Most commercial businesses use a combination of average costs and percentages to highlight areas for action but really, in order to take action you need to look at individual categories by themselves.

Costs aren't always appropriate if sales have risen, whereas percentages only look at comparisons not at money amounts. Also, many managers are measured on their departmental cost percentages and a bad result can mean no bonus or a limited pay rise.

Control of costs

We will review these by category (raw materials, labour and other expenses) and consider how they can be controlled within the different sectors. We'll start with raw materials as these have the most stages to go through before the product is consumed. Labour is of course a part of this too but has fewer stages to go through where controls are needed. The other costs will be reviewed last as, although they aren't usually as significant as the others, they still need to be effectively managed. You'll see some more relevant ratios and we will then discuss potential problems and suggest some solutions (there's more in other chapters).

Small businesses often have very few types of costs (a guesthouse, for instance only offers a room and breakfast, and perhaps dinner) and these should be easy to control, especially if the owner is also the manager. Even here, however, there will be opportunities to trim costs, perhaps by the use of flexible labour and the purchase of food only when it is needed. Also, wherever there are fewer products for sale the cost control is likely to be simpler as there are fewer items, and possibly fewer staff, to manage.

Raw materials

As mentioned in Chapter 2, raw materials are 'cost of sales'. We will mainly concentrate on food and beverages but others (such as telephone) will be discussed as well.

Ratios for raw materials

As we've seen, these costs are usually variable and so are directly proportional to the number of meals (or drinks) that are provided for customers, whether for money or not. The main two ratios that are used are cost of food or beverage per customer and the food or beverage cost percentage.

Food cost per customer
(or any other)
$$= \frac{\text{Total food cost}}{\text{Number of customers}} \quad \text{£p}$$

Cost per meal
(if more than one meal per person, such as on a long-haul flight, in a residential home or on a package break)
$$= \frac{\text{Total cost for meal}}{\text{Number of meals}} \quad \text{£p}$$

Cost per person (or meal) is used extensively in cost sector catering where there is a specific amount allowed per meal or per day – and this may be subsidized. It's less popular in commercial environments where they are more likely to use percentages. The chef on a cruise ship normally has a budget of a food cost per passenger per day to feed the vast number and variety of meals that are served during the day – all included in the price of the cruise. This can be up to seven meals a day (does anybody eat that much?).

$$\text{Food cost percentage (also beverage, tobacco, telephone, laundry and so on)} = \frac{\text{Food cost of sales}}{\text{Food sales}} \%$$

$$\text{Beverage gross profit (also food and others, as above)} = \frac{\text{Beverage gross profit}}{\text{Beverage sales}} \%$$

These are the most important percentages of all for catering areas and show the cost of the raw materials consumed (or the GP – which depends on the focus of the business) in relation to the sales. Different sectors will, of course, work towards different percentages. Some have to achieve the same cost percentage on all items but it is more common to have different percentages for different items. A university food facility (which is subsidized) may have a 60% food cost whereas a pasta restaurant can work to 30%.

Even within a single unit, different meals and dishes can have lower food cost (usually expressed as 'higher GP') – so a hotel breakfast has a much higher GP than lunch, and an orange juice in a café a lower GP than a cup of tea. For an explanation of why this happens then please see Chapter 5, on pricing.

Overall cost averages for your entire stock really aren't good enough as they can hide where a problem occurs. For instance, would you notice a 1% fall in GP if you have a very big turnover – but convert this into money and you will see the value of what you have lost? Here's an example:

Sales for a month	£500,000
Cost of sales at 34%	£170,000
Cost of sales at 35%	£175,000
Difference (Loss!)	£5,000

Five thousand pounds would pay a part-time member of staff for a year.

As an example we can add to the restaurant exercise from the previous chapter.

Note that the cost of sales % (and GP%) on food is calculated as a proportion of food sales (and beverage costs to beverage sales), not total sales.

	Budget	Budget (%)	Actual	Actual (%)	Variance	Variance (%)
Covers sold	1,120	952			(168)	(15.0)
Revenue						
Food	20,100	75.0	17,600	80.4	(2,500)	(12.4)
Beverage	6,700	25.0	4,300	19.6	(2,400)	(35.8)
Total	26,800	100.0	21,900	100.0	(4,900)	(18.3)
Cost of Sales						
Food	(10,000)	(49.8)	(7,900)	(44.9)	2,100	21.0
Beverage	(2,670)	(39.9)	(1,620)	(37.7)	1,050	39.3
Total	(12,670)	(47.3)	(9,520)	(43.5)	3,150	24.9
Gross profit						
Food	10,100	50.2	9,700	55.1	(400)	(4.0)
Beverage	4,030	60.1	2,680	62.3	(1,350)	(33.5)
Total	14,130	52.7	12,380	56.5	(1,750)	(12.4)
Total cost of sales/cover	11.31		10.00		(1.31)	(11.6)
Total gross profit /cover	12.62		13.00		0.39	3.1

Attitudes to control

Attitudes to food by staff can be tricky – do they see it as fuel, as an item they prepare or sell, or as a reward? They may not think of it as having value, and so consider it as consumable.

Mini-case

A well-patronized restaurant used a lot of student labour who were not well paid. They relied on their tips to help them fund their studies, and on the meal that they ate while working.

A new manager wasn't happy, though, when he realized that the staff were eating the very expensive gateaux intended for customers and spoiling the display at the same time. Supplies for guests were running out and these weren't being costed for in the staff meal allowance – result: unhappy guests and a high food cost. He explained to the staff (carefully!) that they weren't entitled to gateaux and that if head office found out they would consider this as stealing. The staff hadn't thought of it this way and certainly hadn't considered the financial implications. They often didn't even eat all the cakes, they just wanted a taste.

A compromise was reached. The staff ate ice-cream as part of the staff meal, and each day they all shared a guest dessert so that they could see what it was like and recommend it to customers.

Attitudes to drink vary by sector. In pubs there's a tradition of staff drinking with customers although many businesses now limit the amount of alcohol consumed as too much of it can affect your ability to do the job. It also costs the business less if staff have soft drinks or water – they're not 'drinking away the profits' any more.

The main problem is that you just can't check everything, as we discussed in the previous chapter. With costs, as with revenue, you have to be able to trust your staff. MBWA helps with costs too, but so does the 'lead from the top' approach. If managers behave honestly and efficiently then most employees will do so too. That said, some types of operation are more susceptible to theft than others – with pubs often being notorious for losses of stock. Some of this is due to drinking on duty, others to the desirability and portability of the product (particularly spirits). It doesn't help when shortfalls on gross profits are called 'shrinkage', which disguises the fact that wastage and fraud may be occurring and that these are controllable.

Ways of improving GPs

We discuss production and portion control further in Chapter 8, on standard costing, and stock usage in Chapter 7 on cash and stocks.

Knowing what's profitable

EPOS systems help you analyse what is selling well and, if programmed with costs for each item, will show you the most and least profitable items and the overall GPs achieved.

You then use your selling skills to persuade people to buy things that have a lower cost, such as own label products or 'specials'. It's most common in food and beverage (it's called *menu engineering*) but is also applicable to other sectors. Remember that you can often achieve a higher GP at different times of day due to *price sensitivity* – you can often charge more for the same item in the evening, for instance, than you can at lunchtime.

Mystery shoppers (mentioned in the last chapter) are often used in bars to monitor not only the sales but also the costs – they'll watch bar staff to see how honest and efficient they are. If it's your own pub then you could ask a friend (who's not known to your staff) to come and be a customer for you and see what's happening.

Mini-case

Buffet crews on one railway line relate how, if the stores staff at their base station forget to load a trolley on their train early in the morning, first-class passengers don't receive their advertised free at-seat trolley service of beverages and biscuits. They then have to be served with standard products, reducing availability for other passengers, which in turn leads to disgruntled passengers and control problems for the crew.

Relationship between costs

One more thing to think about. Sometimes a high food (or beverage) cost can be offset by lower labour costs – so you need to think overall rather than in isolation. Buffet meals are a good example – they are very high in food cost due to the wastage element, but the labour cost is minimal. Buying-in prepared products is expensive on food cost but saves on kitchen labour, and so on.

Mini bars are very expensive staff-wise to replenish on a daily basis so most hotels will only do this after the guest departs. Most guests are honest, but some aren't, and you do need to factor into the cost the loss you will make from some guests. It may be worthwhile trying to identify if particular types of guests are more likely to cheat than others – and targeting their rooms for daily inspections.

Also, hospitals may have volunteers to help on wards with consequent savings on labour. Unfortunately these 'staff' may not have any knowledge of control and so, for instance, give a larger drink of orange juice than is budgeted for.

Other types of 'raw materials'

Telephone units

In a hotel or similar establishments where telephones are installed in rooms the guests are charged a premium rate for the calls they make. This can be several times the cost of using a pay-phone but establishments argue that the charge is subsidizing the cost of providing the switchboard service, and so on.

The cost of the units counts as 'cost of sales' and is expressed as a percentage as are other costs. It's a fully variable cost too – the unit charge is only imposed when a call is made. There are usually minimal losses due to wastage as most establishments have computerized switchboards that automatically charge the call to the guest room. The main losses on telephones are due to staff calls that are accounted for in departmental costs. Cutting costs is largely due to finding a cheaper supplier of whom there are now several available (although it depends where in the country you live – London has far more options than remote rural areas).

Guest laundry and dry-cleaning

This is normally 'contracted out' whereby the items are sent to an external company for cleaning. The company will make a charge to the hotel (or apartment) which then forms the 'cost price'. This is grossed up (see Chapter 5 on pricing on how to do this) to give a selling price which is charged to the guest bill. Again, the only potential savings are in finding a cheaper supplier but here quality of service is more important than cost – to both hotel and guest.

In-house movies

The last area where you can find cost of sales is in-house movies for which most hotels now make a charge. Sometimes you can receive a movie 'free' but it's usually a couple of years old and you've probably seen it before. Again the charge to the guest includes the equipment rental and may well subsidize the provision of cable channels, for instance. The main problem with these is guests admitting that they have actually watched a movie and trying to have the charge taken off their bill (especially if it's an adult movie, surprisingly…). Nowadays you have to press an 'accept' button on the TV control to watch the movie, or it will disconnect, and this has minimized the problems.

(By the way, you can ask the hotel reception to bar the adult movies if you don't want your kids to watch them).

Labour

Payroll can be the biggest expense of all – in some sectors such as hospital cleaning it can represent 90% of the total costs. Even in commercial catering it can represent 30% of sales. There are some controls that you can put in place but often there is a minimum staffing requirement due to health and safety legislation, hygiene rules or standards of service.

Much payroll is fixed in nature, with staff being employed on permanent contracts, particularly in the UK. Other countries often have more 'flexible' approaches to contracts, and there's a trend towards these in some sectors here too. Part of the problem though is the different attitudes of staff and management – what managers see as flexible working a staff member may see as exploitation.

Ratios

Here are the main ratios that are used to measure overall payroll cost:

Payroll percentage $= \dfrac{\text{Payroll cost}}{\text{Sales}}$ %

Payroll cost per customer $= \dfrac{\text{Payroll cost}}{\text{Customers}}$ £p

These are similar to the ratios we've already looked at. The last, non-monetary, type of ratio is productivity. We've seen that you can calculate a payroll cost or percentage, but you can also look at staffing in terms of time. Here's a couple of examples:

Time taken to serve a customer $= \dfrac{\text{Number of customers}}{\text{Time}}$ *expressed as minutes and seconds*

Meals per labour hour
(used a lot in cost sector catering) $= \dfrac{\text{Number of meals}}{\text{Number of hours}}$

Here you are seeing the average time taken to do a job. You might also want to see how many tasks a person does in a day:

Rooms cleaned per staff member $= \dfrac{\text{Number of rooms}}{\text{Number of staff}}$

Meals prepared per staff member $= \dfrac{\text{Number of meals}}{\text{Number of staff}}$

For example – if you have 5 staff preparing 2000 sandwiches a day then the ratio would be:

Sandwiches prepared per staff member $= \dfrac{\text{Number of meals}}{\text{Number of staff}}$ $\dfrac{2000}{5}$ = 400 each

Fixed payroll

This generally means the salaries and wages of all permanent staff which in many businesses is the majority of employees, whether full or part time. They are often perceived as more stable and more reliable than 'casual' staff which is good for maintaining service standards but can be difficult cost-wise. Also, the higher the grade of establishment the more likely there is to be more permanent, fixed staffing – and so payroll cost.

Pay rates in different areas of the country vary (for the same job) and accordingly will also affect the payroll costs although now, with minimum wage regulations, the variance may not be as great as previously. In sectors such as cruise-lines, staff tend to be employed from nations where pay rates are lower than some western countries, which can also reduce costs.

Given the high proportion of fixed payroll in many sectors, managing the cost can be tricky. There are things you can do, however:

▷ Use of forecasting techniques to predict the level of business can help you to schedule staff more efficiently. If you know, for instance, that you are likely to have a quiet period ahead then you can persuade staff to take holidays or bank holidays that they are owed.

▷ Some types of business have traditional peaks and troughs at different times of year. For instance, pubs and restaurants tend to be very busy in the weeks leading up to Christmas so staff have little time off. In the New Year, however, they can be much quieter and so the staff can take the time that they are owed.

▷ If you are able to negotiate with your staff you can offer to give them time off in lieu rather than pay overtime, so that they can take several days 'holiday' off together.

▷ If a member of staff leaves, do you have to replace them immediately? If business looks quieter then you may be able to manage without that post for a couple of months or so (for management positions it may take you that long to recruit anyway).

▷ You can employ new members of staff on lower pay rates – but you need to be very careful here. Sometimes this can be legitimate if the leaver was entitled to long-service bonuses or enhancement but if the business is unionized then there may well be an agreed rate for each job. There are now established precedents that mean that staff should maintain terms and conditions when new caterers take over a contract.

▷ One other approach is to keep a minimum permanent staff and then ask them to work overtime when it's busy. You need to recognize though that staff are often more efficient if they work shorter hours – working overtime (paid or unpaid) just makes them tired and less efficient. This applies to you too!

Part time and flexible payroll

There are two approaches to flexible working – flexible jobs and flexible hours:

Flexible jobs have always been used in smaller units but in recent years has become more prevalent in larger units. Everybody may now be multi-skilled so that they can help out where needed.

Mini-case

A large hotel situated next to a premier division football club tends to get very busy on match days. When this happens all the managers are expected to help the bar staff clear glasses and change ashtrays. Once the match has started the room attendants join the porters in cleaning the floor, toilets and tables so that the area will look 'normal' again as quickly as possible.

This isn't seen as just work – it's everybody pulling together for the benefit of all. Staff enjoy doing different jobs occasionally.

You can offer *flexible hours* on a permanent or non-permanent (short-term contract) basis. This can be very efficient in keeping costs under control when you have variable levels of business (but note that the entitlement for benefits may now be the same as for permanent and full-time staff). You have to balance this flexibility with staff morale – if staff are happy with this type of contract then it may be the best solution but there is a danger that they may become demoralized and leave for more stable employment.

Students, for instance, frequently work during their holiday periods or at weekends on short-term contracts to fill in while permanent staff are on holiday or days off. Working parents often need hours to fit in child-care and so you can often juggle different types of workforce at different times.

Lower grade establishments tend to operate with more flexible payroll – staff on variable contracts who move jobs frequently. Although this means that you can control the costs more easily (e.g. not hiring when you don't need them) there's a trade-off in lack of reliability and levels of skills. Skilled staff are more likely to want (and be able to secure) permanent employment with good benefits and career prospects. Fast food takeaways often advertise for staff for a limited number of hours per day – say to cover lunch-time peaks. They can't afford to employ staff who aren't busy.

▶▶ **ACTIVITY**

Do you know of any businesses that operate with a flexible workforce? Look out on the high street for advertisements for staff – they will often say 'hours to suit – from 2 to 30 hours per week' or similar. They look like they're being flexible for the employee, but really it's to help manage their payroll cost.

Contracting out or outsourcing labour

This can be approached through de-skilling, contract labour or casuals.

De-skilling

A lot of kitchens have also 'contracted out' the preparation of food items and now buy in items such as meat pre-prepared. Few kitchens have a full pastry section now – they buy their cakes from specialist bakers. The cost is higher but there is a saving on payroll costs and on the space required. Although there are benefits for the business there's a danger the chefs themselves may feel under-used and undervalued if their skills are no longer necessary.

Contract staff

You can hire staff in from an agency to do a variety of jobs, or hire a firm for a particular area. Agency staff can work in housekeeping, administration, on food counters and as drivers. You might hire a specialist company to clean your carpets, maintain your electrical or catering equipment or to run your accounts or technology. This is often known as *outsourcing*. The supplier contracts to provide the service and you have to pay the bill. Although expensive it can be cost-effective especially if you need technical expertise.

Casual staff

These are the traditional way of managing payroll in a variable-volume situation. The most common area is in banqueting where staff are hired purely for a specific function but may also used to fill in gaps when regular staff are on holiday or sick. Many may be hired via an agency but this can be expensive so a unit may have its own list of casual staff it can call if needed. Event catering peaks in the summer for outdoor events and for these few weeks you may have a team of casuals who work on a series of functions.

Casuals used to work for cash-in-hand and so paid little tax, but now the Inland Revenue insists that they are paid via the payroll and have tax deducted so that they are 'legal employees'. The more formal nature of their employment has meant a more stable workforce with casuals now being considered as part of the staff, albeit often with irregular hours. Costs have increased (for pay, uniforms, meals, etc.) but so has the quality of service.

Employee Benefits

Payroll cost isn't just the cost of the wages – there are all the 'benefits' (or 'on-cost') that have to be added to the overall cost of employing someone. The cost of this averages about 20% – less for a part-timer and more for a manager. Another payroll ratio that may be relevant is the percentage of benefits to basic pay. Examples of benefit are:

Holiday pay	Sick pay
Maternity pay	Paternity pay
Parental leave	Subsidized child care
Bonuses	Pension contributions
National Insurance (another employment tax)	Life assurance
Travel home late at night	Staff accommodation
Staff meals	Subsidized loans for travel or mortgages
Company cars	Mobile phones
Private health care	Uniforms
Subsidized or free laundry or dry cleaning	

▶▶ ACTIVITY

What sort of benefits do you have? Is it just meals on duty, a uniform, holiday and sick pay or are there more?

A manager employed overseas on an 'ex-pat' package can have a benefits package larger than their salary. This can include annual travel for the whole family back to their home country, housing, school fees, company cars and so on – it gets VERY expensive to employ ex-pats, so you have to be sure that they are worth it.

Training

The cost of training can be regarded in different ways. To some it's a benefit, and so it classed as part of payroll. To other businesses it's an overall business cost as training affects all areas. It can be thought of as very controllable, and in difficult trading periods is often one of the first costs to be cut. BUT... there's loads of (often anecdotal) evidence to suggest that better trained employees bring in better sales and costs. On one hand employers complain that 'they can't get the trained staff' and yet with the other don't put the investment into staff training. You'll see frequent letters and articles about this topic if you read the trade press regularly.

There's a tendency to concentrate on health and safety and fire training (the ones required by law) and leave other training to just 'happen'. Staff then vote with their feet – if they aren't invested in (that is, trained and developed) then they won't stay. This is considered more in the final chapter. Training is crucial to ensure good cost control. This can be in terms of attitude (zero tolerance of theft, for instance) or in skills such as cleaning silver and glassware (which can be very expensive and easily breakable), portion control or use of paper goods.

Other costs

You have seen the overall cost per customer and cost percentages that were calculated earlier. You can use these formulas to calculate individual costs too. Costs for departments are calculated as a percentage of the departmental sales, but for administration as a percentage of the total unit sales.

Again costs are split into fixed and variable and we will consider some of the types of costs that occur in each of these classifications. Remember though that cost behaviour differs by sector (and sometimes by season) and so what may be classified as variable in one situation may be fixed in another. As we've seen, in general the higher the 'grade' of business the more fixed costs they have in order to maintain their established standards.

Variable costs

You need to establish exactly which costs are variable in your business and then decide how much you need to spend on each item – this is part of setting standards. This is likely to be dependent on actual items so you need to work out what you need as well as how much it will cost. So – how many paper napkins do you need on average per customer? Is it one each, or do they take more? What quality – one ply is far cheaper, but two ply feels more luxurious – three ply even more so? Do you give straws with your soft drinks? How many tablets of soap does each guest need? How many times do you change the sheets (every day in a five star hotel but only on departure in a guest house)? Do you need branded products – they may be expensive but they are also a marketing technique.

You can calculate these costs individually by customer or by percentage as well. For example:

$$\text{Paper cost percentage} = \frac{\text{Paper cost}}{\text{Sales}} \ \%$$

$$\text{Paper cost per customer} = \frac{\text{Paper cost}}{\text{Customers}} \ \text{£p}$$

Once your standards are established you need to communicate this to your staff so they know too – and then monitor that this is happening. If different rules apply to different types of customers then this needs to be clear too (business guests get shampoo and conditioner in their rooms but tour groups only get shampoo; the directors dining room has linen tablecloths AND napkins AND silver cutlery but everybody else has bare tables and stainless steel cutlery).

Rent

One more cost that may sometimes be variable is rent. If you pay a fixed rental (probably based on a square metre basis) then this counts as a fixed cost. If, however, your rent is based on a percentage of sales then it is fully variable. Management contracts often operate in this way and so do retail or catering units in shopping centres and airports. The rent can be as high as 25% of revenue in some cases.

Fixed costs

Many departmental costs are fixed as we saw earlier. You need to keep the lighting and heating on in your building whenever you are open, and floors in a cafeteria or hostel need cleaning every day. Even if a hospital ward is 'closed' it still needs some attention to keep it clean. Motorway service areas are another example, they don't just operate the catering outlets but have to offer all the other facilities on the site, on a 24-hour basis – the shops, toilets, parking, petrol and amusements. The costs of running these are nearly all fixed – it doesn't matter whether it's the middle of the night or the middle of the day they still need to be open for business. Event caterers need to transport all equipment and materials to the location, which incurs fixed costs such as refrigeration, electricity and running costs for the van. These may vary with the size and distance to the event but are still essentially fixed in nature.

Managing costs

You can try to manage fixed costs to some extent – often by planning ahead. By finding the cheapest place to purchase your products you may be able to cut costs. For instance, using an alternative supplier for utilities (electricity, gas, water or telephone) may help you to trim the cost. You can also consider using a lower specification (such as lower strength light bulbs) or look long-term and try to save costs by installing new equipment or changing behaviour. Again with utilities, modern boiler systems can cut energy usage dramatically, and training staff to only switch on gas ovens when needed saves costs as well as helping the environment.

Recycling, while also environmentally friendly is also financially beneficial. In the past there has been extensive wastage of all types of resource within the unit. By re-using and recycling you can save costs as well. You can re-use paper for message pads, recycle bottles and cans and cut down on printing by keeping most records electronically rather than hard-copy. You can cut old large linen tablecloths into smaller ones, and then into napkins and eventually they can get used up for kitchen cloths.

Seasonality

Some businesses are highly seasonal which affects their cost structures. Traditionally many seaside hotels used to close in winter due to low occupancies but now tend to remain open and to look for new markets that will generate some revenue to cover their fixed operating costs. Apartment complexes and large hotels in resort areas can offer economies of scale in that a relatively small management team can operate a large number of room blocks and other facilities. Operative staff may be hired on a flexible, perhaps seasonal, basis so the opportunity is available to open and close different areas according to demand.

Contracting out

It can be cheaper to 'contract out' (outsource) some services as well as payroll, and certainly easier. Bedlinen and table linen, for instance, often used to be done 'in-house' which can still be cost effective if you have the facilities. Most of this is contracted out now to specialists because of the problems in hiring trained staff, the space that is required and the environmental issues associated with chemicals and water. For very small businesses (like a bed and breakfast) it still may be quicker to do it yourself on a domestic washer, but for larger units the volumes of linen required are enormous (think about a 500-person banquet and the napkins and cloths required, and then the need for the same again the next day).

Cleaning of public areas is also often contracted out to specialist cleaners who visit at quiet times (often the middle of the night). There have been some experiments with contracting out cleaning on a large scale and these have been successful in some areas (such as hospitals and schools) but less so in hotels. This may be because of the higher quality of furnishings or because of the nature of the business (open 24 hours, for instance).

▶▶ **ACTIVITY** ═══════════════════════════════════

Are any of your services contracted out in any way? Can you identify why this is?
═══

Exercise

Using the Restaurant exercise again, let's add some more costs. Please calculate the profit and percentages as well.

Profit & Loss Report – Restaurant   28-day period

	Budget		Actual		Variance	%
Seats available	50		50			
Seats per period	1400		1400		0	0.0
Covers sold	1,120		952		(168)	(15.0)
Revenue	(£)	(%)	(£)	(%)	(£)	(%)
Food	20,100	75.0	17,600	80.4	(2,500)	(12.4)
Beverage	6,700	25.0	4,300	19.6	(2,400)	(35.8)
Total	26,800	100.0	21,900	100.0	(4,900)	(18.3)
Cost of sales						
Food	(10,000)	(49.8)	(7,900)	(44.9)	2,100	21.00
Beverage	(2,670)	(39.9)	(1,620)	(37.7)	1,050	39.3
Total	(12,670)	(47.3)	(9,520)	(43.5)	3,150	24.9

Gross profit

	Budget (£)	Budget (%)	Actual (£)	Actual (%)	Variance (£)	Variance (%)
Food	10,100	50.2	9,700	55.1	(400)	(4.0)
Beverage	4,030	60.1	2,680	62.3	(1,350)	(33.5)
Total	14,130	52.7	12,380	56.5	(1,750)	(12.4)
Payroll cost	(9,520)		(8,400)		1,120	
Departmental expenses	(2,100)		(1,600)		500	
Food and beverage profit						
Payroll cost per cover						
Expenses cost per cover						
Profit per cover						

The answer:

Profit & Loss Report – Restaurant   28-day period

	Budget		Actual		Variance	%
Seats available	50		50			
Seats per period	1400		1400		0	0.0
Covers sold	1,120		952		(168)	(15.0)
Revenue	(£)	(%)	(£)	(%)	(£)	(%)
Food	20,100	75.0	17,600	80.4	(2,500)	(12.4)
Beverage	6,700	25.0	4,300	19.6	(2,400)	(35.8)
Total	26,800	100.0	21,900	100.0	(4,900)	(18.3)
Cost of sales						
Food	(10,000)	(49.8)	(7,900)	(44.9)	2,100	21.00
Beverage	(2,670)	(39.9)	(1,620)	(37.7)	1,050	39.3
Total	(12,670)	(47.3)	(9,520)	(43.5)	3,150	24.9
Gross profit						
Food	10,100	50.2	9,700	55.1	(400)	(4.0)
Beverage	4,030	60.1	2,680	62.3	(1,350)	(33.5)
Total	14,130	52.7	12,380	56.5	(1,750)	(12.4)
Payroll cost	(9,520)	(35.5)	(8,400)	(38.4)	1,120	11.8
Departmental expenses	(2,100)	(7.8)	(1,600)	(7.3)	500	23.8
Food and beverage profit	2,510	9.4	2,380	10.9	130	5.2

Average spend/cover – food	17.95	18.49	0.54	3.0
Average spend/cover – beverage	5.98	4.52	(1.47)	(24.5)
Total cost of sales/cover	11.31	10.00	(1.31)	(11.6)
Total gross profit/cover	12.62	13.00	0.39	3.1
Payroll cost per cover	8.50	8.82	0.32	(3.8)
Expenses cost per cover	1.88	1.68	0.19	(10.4)
Profit per cover	2.24	2.50	0.26	11.6
Seat occupancy %	80.0%	68.0%	(12.0%)	(15.0%)

What do all these figures mean? Look at these:

▷ Is there any relationship between the average spends for food and for beverage?

▷ What about the cost of food amounts? The average costs look less, but what about the percentage?

▷ Is payroll cost 'good' or 'bad' – and from whose perspective? Is there a relationship between payroll and Cost of sales, for instance?

▷ What about other expenses?

▷ Lastly, what about profit?

Fixed charges

These really can be difficult to manage and you do need to think a long way ahead if you are to minimize these costs. Here are some ideas:

▷ Interest payments (see cash management) – it may be possible to negotiate a lower rate

▷ Rent can be re-negotiated – and do you really need an expensive high-street location anyway? Must you provide staff accommodation in rented houses, or can you find an alternative?

▷ Depreciation is based on buying fixed assets. For the future, could equipment be leased or hired? This will help your cash situation as well as reducing the depreciation (though you'd still have rental costs).

▷ It may be possible to get business rates may be able to be reduced, with negotiation, if you can prove that they are higher than equivalent businesses in the area.

▶▶ **ACTIVITY**

Find three expense items in your area that you think could be better managed in terms of cost. Suggest these to your manager. There may be other reasons that you aren't aware of for high costs, but at least this will develop your awareness.

Here's another exercise. Do the figures, then look at what they mean. Focus on the payroll and the cost of sales, and try and see what's happening.

Town Centre Department Store

	March (£)	(%)	April (£)	(%)	May (£)	(%)
Sales						
Café	6,000		7,000		8,000	
Restaurant	8,000		10,000		14,000	
Total						
Cost of Sales						
Café	(3,000)		(3,780)		(4,560)	
Restaurant	(3,200)		(4,200)		(6,020)	
Total						
Gross Profit						
Café	3,000		3,220		3,440	
Restaurant	4,800		5,800		7,980	
Total						
Wages	(3,500)		(3,905)		(2,990)	
Overtime	(300)		(355)		(1,410)	
Net profit						
Covers						
Café	3,750		4,667		5,714	
Restaurant	1,667		2,128		3,043	
Total						
Average spends						
Café						
Restaurant						
Total						
Gross profit/cover						
Café						
Restaurant						
Total						

Wages/cover					
Overtime/cover					
Net profit/cover					

Here's the answer:

Town Centre Department Store

	March		April		May	
	(£)	(%)	(£)	(%)	(£)	(%)
Sales						
Café	6,000	42.9	7,000	41.2	8,000	36.4
Restaurant	8,000	57.1	10,000	58.8	14,000	63.6
Total	14,000	100.0	17,000	100.0	22,000	100.0
Cost of Sales						
Café	(3,000)	50.0	(3,780)	54.9	(4,560)	57.0
Restaurant	(3,200)	40.0	(4,200)	42.0	(6,020)	43.0
Total	(6,200)	44.3	(7,980)	46.9	(10,580)	48.1
Gross Profit						
Café	3,000	50.0	3,220	46.0	3,440	43.0
Restaurant	4,800	60.0	5,800	58.0	7,980	57.0
Total	7,800	55.7	9,020	53.1	11,420	51.9
Wages	(3,500)	25.0	(3,905)	23.0	(2,990)	13.6
Overtime	(300)	2.1	(355)	2.1	(1,410)	6.4
Net profit	4,000	28.6	4,760	28.0	7,020	31.9
Covers						
Café	3,750		4,667		5,714	
Restaurant	1,667		2,128		3,043	
Total	5,417		6,795		8,757	
Average spends	(£)		(£)		(£)	
Café	1.60		1.50		1.40	
Restaurant	4.80		4.70		4.60	
Total	2.58		2.50		2.51	
Gross profit/cover						
Café	0.80		0.69		0.60	
Restaurant	2.88		2.73		2.62	
Total	1.44		1.33		1.30	
Wages/cover	0.65		0.57		0.34	
Overtime/cover	0.06		0.05		0.16	
Net profit/cover	0.74		0.70		0.80	

By the way – the total average spend is the total revenue divided by total covers – it's *not* calculated by averaging the two spends as you can't 'average an average'. That's why it might look slightly odd.

Look at the month to month changes in payroll and GPs and consider how they might affect each other. Has the approach to food purchasing changed, do you think?

Summary

In this chapter we've looked at the principles of managing costs. You have:

▷   Reviewed the differences between fixed and variable costs and identified some within your own area

▷   Discussed how different costs are classified

▷   Calculated ratios that assist in controlling costs

▷   Discussed the role of the manager in controlling costs

▷   Identified some specific ways in which the manager can control raw materials, labour and other costs.

Quiz

1.   What's a variable cost?
2.   What's a fixed cost?
3.   Why is it important to know the difference?
4.   What are the main ratios used for food and beverage cost?
5.   What's the most important cost in cleaning a hospital ward? Can you reduce this cost easily?
6.   How do you calculate productivity?

5

Pricing to achieve profit

▼
▼
▼
▼
▼

Introduction

One of the most important techniques for managers to understand is how to price a product to attract customers – and also to achieve a profit (or at least cover all the costs). If you can be aware of all the different factors that influence a price (and not just what the customer is prepared to pay) then you will be able to generate both revenue and profit from your products and services. Another helpful technique is to know how many you need to sell of a product or service at a given price to cover all the costs – this is called the 'Break-Even-Point'.

By the end of this section you will be able to:

▷   Describe the factors that influence pricing decisions

▷   Identify the most appropriate pricing method for a product or service

▷   Calculate a price to achieve a profit

▷   Calculate how many you need to sell to reach the break-even point.

Different types of pricing

There are two different approaches used in pricing – which can be generally described as the 'accountant's method' and the 'marketer's method'. Traditionally the two are seen as totally different, but we will try and make them fit together in order to satisfy the needs of both. We'll also look briefly at putting package prices together. We will look at the 'accountant's method' first, which uses costs as the basis for calculating a selling price. This is known as 'cost-plus'.

One item to note: the selling price is the price the business receives and does not include any VAT (Value Added Tax), which needs to be added on afterwards to give a 'price charged to the customer' which you would display on a menu or tariff board.

Cost-plus pricing

For this method the most important factor is the costs identified with producing the product and then a margin, or 'mark-up' is added on to cover all other costs and the profit to arrive at the selling price. There are three main types of cost-plus pricing – gross profit, contribution margin and bottom-up methods.

Gross profit method

This is the most common method used in pricing food and beverage products, but is very simplistic in its approach. It uses only the cost of the raw materials and the margin that is added covers all other costs (variable and fixed) and the profit required. Look at Figure 5.1.

Figure 5.1 Gross profit pricing

The margin is the same as the GP achieved – hence the name – and is normally quoted as a percentage of the selling price, e.g. a pint of beer:

Cost of beer	£0.70	35.0%
Margin (GP)	£1.30	65.0%
Selling price	£2.00	100.0%

(If you then added VAT at 17.5% you'd have a price to the customer of £2.35 – more than three times the actual cost of the beer. For wines in restaurants it's quite common to pay four or five times the amount you would pay in a supermarket for the same bottle of wine.)

TIP

To add VAT at 17.5% on to a selling price to reach the 'menu price' or 'price charged to the customer', take the selling price and multiply it by 1.175 – that gives you the final number you need. The amount of VAT is the difference between the first and the second figures.

There are no 'standard' cost percentages for products – it will vary according to the type of operation, location and so on. You'll see this more when we look at market-based pricing.

▶▶ ACTIVITY

Look at your operation (or one you know) – do they use this type of pricing?

Contribution margin method

GP pricing only uses the raw materials – and ignores all other variable costs such as wages, paper goods, give-aways, linen, transport and so on (these are covered by the margin, mentioned above). A better approach would be to take all of the variable costs into the calculation – this is called contribution pricing. Here the 'cost base' is all the variable costs, which we discussed earlier. Using this method the margin then covers the fixed costs and the profit required (see Figure 5.2).

▼
▼
▼

Figure 5.2 Contribution pricing

You can use this method where you have a lot of variable costs – such as a fast-food operation, a day trip or a package holiday. For example, for a burger bar:

	(£)	(%)
Variable Costs – burger, bun, sauce, garnish, packaging, labour and so on	0.90	60.0
Contribution	0.60	40.0
Selling price	1.50	100.0

Where the business has a wide range of products this method is still feasible. A theme park, for example, may have lots of rides, retail shops, food outlets and vending machines but should still be able to identify all the different variable costs associated with each type. The only minor drawback of both these methods is that they assume that the cost of the individual items will be the same – which is also unrealistic. Given that items such as food change their cost daily it is inevitable that the profit will change daily too – and so the GP or contribution achieved is only an average over a period and can't be considered totally accurate.

Again, do you use this method? Would it be more appropriate than GP pricing? Can you think of any other product or service that could use it?

Different types of pricing

Here's one to practise:

Pricing a take-away coffee

Number sold	5,000
Food cost per cup	£0.20
Labour cost per cup	£0.15
Paper and other supplies per cup	£0.05
Fixed costs (total)	£3,000
Profit required	£500

What price should be charged, including VAT?

You can do this two ways. The easiest is to work out the fixed cost per cup, the profit per cup, then add all the costs and profit together to reach a selling price. Then you would add the VAT. Alternatively you could multiply out the number of cups times the food cost, paper cost and so on to get the total costs, and then divide that by the number of cups to reach a per item price. Here's a grid for the first method (fill in the boxes, please):

Coffees

	Total	Per cup
Fixed costs	£3,000	
Profit required	£500	
Variable costs		
Food	£0.20	
Labour	£0.15	
Paper	£0.05	
Add all these together to get a selling price:		

To get a menu price, you need to add VAT.
Take the selling price and multiply it by 1.175.

You could check it works by multiplying it all out to see if you reach the profit that you require.

Sales
Variable costs
Contribution
Fixed costs
Net profit

Here's the answer:

	Total	
Coffees		5,000
	Total	Per cup
Fixed costs	£3,000	£0.60
Profit required	£500	£0.10
Variable costs		
Food		£0.20
Labour		£0.15
Paper		£0.05
Selling price		£1.10
Plus VAT		£1.29

Let's hope it's a good cup of coffee at this price!

Grossing up

Sometimes you just have the cost amount and you need to achieve a certain contribution percentage (or GP percentage). For this you need to gross up the cost amount to reach the selling price.

What if you had a £23.50 variable cost and wanted to achieve an 80% contribution on sales?

- the variable percentage is 20% (selling price = 100% less contribution 80%)

If you DIVIDE the cost by the percentage that it represents you will find out the gross amount

TIP

To divide by a percentage, using a calculator (and the figures in the example below) press '23.50', then the divide button, then '20' and finally the '%' button. This gives you a figure of 117.50.

So the selling price (before VAT) will be:

$$\frac{\text{Variable Cost}}{\text{Variable Cost \%}} = \frac{£23.50}{20\%} = £117.50 \text{ selling price}$$

Assume you had a £4.75 laundry cost and wanted to achieve a 35% cost of sales. What is the selling price?

- this £4.75 cost represents 35% of the selling price (which = 100%).

So:

$$\frac{\text{Cost price}}{\text{Cost \%}} = \frac{£4.75}{35\%} = £13.57 \text{ selling price} = £15.95$$

price (includes VAT)
on the guest laundry list

(You can check it back – deduct the VAT to get to the selling price. Take the £13.57 and multiply it by 35% to see the laundry cost in £).

TIP

To deduct VAT from a customer price:

Take the customer price and DIVIDE it by 1.175 to get back to the selling price – the reverse of adding the VAT as you did before.

Here's another price to try:

A guest house has variable costs of £20.25 and wants to achieve a contribution of 32%. What's the selling price – and the price charged to the customer?

Answer:

$$\frac{\text{Variable Cost}}{\text{Variable Cost \%}} = \frac{£20.25}{68\%} = £29.78 \text{ selling price} = £34.99 \text{ including VAT (say £35)}$$

Bottom Up method

The last cost-plus method is known as 'bottom-up' pricing (also as the Hubbart formula). It is mainly used for new projects, particularly hotels, where you need to know in advance whether you will achieve the required return (profit) on your investment.

The best description is that it is an 'upside-down' P&L report, and it is almost always used by consultants when looking at 'new builds'. They use standard average costs from published industry reports (such as TriHospitality, 2001) so that they can compare one project to another. Within an existing business you might want to use this for a refurbishment project, for instance, or an extension, in which case your accounts office should have figures available.

To calculate it (this example is for a new hotel) you need to start with the profit you want, add back the tax and then the costs until you reach the revenue needed (subtracting any secondary departments on the way). Once you have the revenue you can divide this by the expected rooms sold to reach an average room rate.

Here's a grid layout:

	Return on investment required	
+	Tax payable	
=	PROFIT BEFORE TAX	_____
+	Fixed costs	
+	Administration & other cost	_____
=	DEPARTMENTAL OPERATING PROFIT	
-	Food & Beverage dept profit	
-	Sundry dept profit	_____
=	ROOMS DEPARTMENT PROFIT	
+	Rooms expenses	_____
=	ROOMS REVENUE	_____

Rooms Available x Occupancy % = Rooms sold

$$\frac{\text{Rooms Revenue}}{\text{Rooms Sold}} = \text{Average Room Rate required}$$

The only tricky bit is adding back the tax at the beginning. To do this requires the 'grossing up' technique that we did earlier. Let's try it:

Profit after tax required by the investors (PaT), £2,000,000, and Tax rate 32%.

Using grossing up you need to find the profit before tax (PbT). This will be 100% before the 32% is deducted – and hence the PaT amount will be 68%.

$$\frac{\text{Profit after tax (PaT)}}{\text{Percentage}} \quad \frac{£2,000,000}{68\%} = £2,941,176 \text{ PbT}$$

The difference between the two is £941,176, which equals 32% of the PbT figure. To check it out (right side up this time):

	(£)	(%)
Profit before tax (PbT)	2,941,176	100.0
Less tax	(941,176)	(32.0)
Profit after tax (PaT)	2,000,000	68.0

Here's an exercise to try using this method:

Capital investment	£2,500,000
Profit required (after tax)	20%
Corporation tax	35%
Fixed costs	£600,000
Administration costs	£300,000
F & B & other departmental profit	£30,000
Rooms expenses/room	£4.50
Available rooms/day	76
Occupancy per year	70%

What room rate needs to be charged to achieve the required return on investment for a year?

Rooms available per year	
Times the occupancy	
Rooms sold	

	£
Profit required, after tax (Capital investment x profit %)	
Add back tax (gross up) = Profit before tax	
Add back fixed costs	
Add back administration costs	
= Gross operating profit (GOP)	
Less other departmental profits	
= Rooms profit	
Add back rooms expenses (Rooms sold times amount per room)	
= Rooms revenue required	
= Average room rate (revenue divided by rooms sold)	
Rate plus VAT (multiply by 1.175)	

Here's the answer:

Rooms available	(76 x 365)	27,740
Times the occupancy		70%
Rooms sold		19,418
		(£)
Profit required (after tax)	£2,500,000 x 20%	500,000
= Profit before tax	Divided by 65%	769,231
Add back Fixed costs		600,000
Add back Administration costs		300,000
= Gross operating profit (GOP)		1,669,231
Less other departmental profits		(30,000)
= Rooms profit		1,639,231
Add back Rooms expenses	19,418 x £4.50	87,381
= Rooms revenue required		1,726,672
= Average room rate	1,726,672/19,418	88.92
Rate plus VAT	£88.92 x 1.175	104.48

▶▶ ACTIVITY

Are there any new projects you can identify (in your business, in your area or mentioned in the press) where you think this method might be used? Could you use it for pricing where you're not changing the physical building, say for a new product range?

Marketer's method of pricing

The 'accountant's methods' of pricing only use costs and profits – they don't take into account any market conditions. The price may generate a profit – but will the customer pay it?

Market-based pricing takes the approach that it is the customer that decides the price, depending on the availability of the product, the local economy, competition and so on. Most of the time the pricing is fairly realistic, and does cover the costs, but this may not always be the case. You can see this is action in the supermarkets – compare the price of a tin of baked beans or a loaf of bread. You may find a very low price indeed, particularly of an own-brand product which can in no way cover all the costs. This is a deliberate ploy to attract you to that branch and persuade you to buy their other products as well, which do generate lots of profits. It's called *loss leadership*.

Competition

In general, the greater the competition, the lower the prices you will find. If there isn't competition, prices tend to be high. If you compare the price of a flight from Heathrow to New York (lots of competition) and one to Aberdeen (very little competition) you'll see that you pay almost the same price – but New York is about five times the distance.

In hospitality and tourism, market-based pricing depends on both the season (think about package holiday prices in August against those of September) and on the location and product. For instance, a lodge-style hotel will need to be competitive with other similar businesses in the area, unless they have some unique selling point which gives them the opportunity to charge a premium price. Similarly a leisure centre may be competing with other facilities for exercise classes, children's parties, group swimming lessons, local authority contracts and so on.

Another example might be a pizza restaurant. An independent restaurant would look at the prices being charged by other, similar, businesses in the area and then price themselves either the same or marginally cheaper. However, big chains look at their competition nationally rather than locally – hence the similarity of prices between the major players all around the country. Their prices, therefore, have a national influence rather than local one.

No obvious competition?

Market-based pricing is also used even where there is no immediate obvious competitor – perhaps simply to attract customers at all. A pub in a village may have to offer special beer, snacks and a wide-screen TV screen with cable-network football if it is to compete against a can of supermarket beer and a home video.

▶▶ **ACTIVITY** ══════════════════════════════════

Look in your local area for prices of different hospitality or tourism products such as coffee shops, take-away sandwiches, chips, bed-and-breakfast or pub beer.

Compare the prices for similar products. If one place charges higher prices can you identify why? Is the product worth the higher price? Do the customers get value for money?

Fitting the methods together

If you are to get the best result from both the market price and the costs you need to look at both together. One approach is to 'trim the costs to fit' (Kotas, 1999) so that at least break-even and if possible a profit is made – it is called backward pricing. This means taking both proposed prices – the market price and the cost-based price, and then cutting the costs without affecting the quality of the product or service, too much.

Suppose you were a hotel reservation manager quoting for a tour group who require a room and breakfast for two nights, for 60 people – a sizeable group for which you have space but whom you know are looking for a very competitive price.

Your normal costs are, per room, per night:

	(£)
Room labour	10.50
Room linen	1.70
Guest supplies	0.65
Breakfast	1.70
Total	14.55

You would normally require a 75% contribution on this booking so the rate would be:

$$\frac{\text{Variable costs}}{\text{Cost \%}} = \frac{£14.55}{25\%} = £58.20$$

But this is too high – they won't pay more than £50. Suppose you normally change the sheets every day, but for this group were to only change them on departure. This would cut the linen costs to £1.00 per room and the labour costs by another pound. The figures would then be:

$$\frac{\text{Variable costs}}{\text{Cost \%}} = \frac{£12.85}{25\%} = £51.40$$

You then need to consider whether there would be any additional revenue from this group. If you could persuade them to eat dinner in the restaurant, generating more profit (especially if they could eat at 18.30 when you are normally quiet) then you could consider offering a lower rate – say £49.00.

Quality

You always need to ensure that the quality of the product is maintained. In the above example you were actually cutting the service but you can assume that the tour group wouldn't be comparing notes with other guests as to whether their beds were changed and other guests were not. It's not acceptable to cut standards where they are visible – say by offering a sub-standard meal.

►► ACTIVITY ‗‗‗‗‗‗‗‗‗‗‗‗‗‗‗‗‗‗‗‗‗‗‗‗‗

Think about times when you've been offered the same product as someone else – but paid a higher rate for it (e.g. a cut-price airline or train ticket). How did you feel?

Offering discounts

Discounting means lowering prices for a short period of time. Again you can see the supermarkets doing it by offering a pound off on a bottle of wine, or 'buy-one-get-second-half-price'. This is done for two main reasons:

▷ As a loss leader, which we've mentioned earlier

▷ To attract customers at a time of low volumes so as to cover some of the costs.

The important point here is that you offer a discount OFF a price – not reduce the price permanently. This means that the price can go back to normal at the end of the promotion without customers getting upset.

The accounting side of pricing would say that you always must charge a price to cover variable costs so you can't discount down below the cost price. You may want to change your method of service, or portion size, to ensure that costs are reduced too. Marketing people say that, as long as sales in other areas will compensate, you can go as low as you wish.

▶▶ ACTIVITY ━━━━━━━━━━━━━━━━━━━━━━━━━━━━━━━━━

Think of a range of discounts you've seen offered recently – in the supermarket, a restaurant, a clothes shop, a hotel or perhaps an electrical supplier. Can you identify WHY the discount was offered? Would the reduced prices still cover costs or are there conditions attached which actually make you spend money elsewhere in the establishment? Would this technique work in your business?

━━━

Other factors to consider

Price and volume

Think about the relationship of price to volume as higher prices may put people off, and vice-versa. Are you happy with more people – can you cope with them? If volume reduces, would this affect your staffing plans?

Covering fixed costs

At certain times (of day, of year) you may also need to attract customers rather than focusing on average spend. This is because the fixed costs have to be paid for and any contribution is better than none.

For instance a theme park will cut its prices substantially off-season (and mid-week) when there is far less demand, just to attract visitors. Once there you are 'captured' and might then buy a meal and probably something from the shop – all with high profit margins. Restaurants offer special, fixed-price menus for the same reason – and also hope that you will return one evening for a more expensive meal.

Value for money

This is as important for a five-star as a one-star product. At the lower levels the perception is that you 'get what you pay for' – but you still need to be good, albeit at a limited-service level. You want to keep your customers, not frighten them away. At the 'five-star' end of the market price is also seen as an indicator of the quality – the higher the price the higher the standard of product and service the customers will expect. If you are in this environment – do you offer perceived value for money?

The perception of value for money can vary for the same person in different scenarios. A business customer may have totally different expectations when on an expense account as opposed to spending their own money. You yourself may react differently in an expensive pub compared to a cheaper one or even if you are on holiday as opposed to going out after work. It's all about expectation, and managers need to make sure they offer the customer what they expect, or better.

Price sensitivity

This means how easy or how difficult it is to change prices – and different sectors, and products, react differently here. Five-star and first-class services are not price sensitive – customers are unlikely to object to minor changes. However, high-street fast food chains are very price sensitive, customers reacting instantly and changing to another provider if the price is increased more than considered reasonable. Even where there is a captive market, for instance on a train, customers may opt not to buy (or bring their own supplies) if the product is considered too expensive.

Price elasticity

This recognizes that the demand for products and services may vary – which can affect the price to be charged. For example, where there is a single resort complex the guests have little choice as to where they will eat – they have to stay within it and accept the prices charged. Similarly students on-campus will also have little choice if they wish to buy a hot meal. This is *inelastic demand* – there is little competition except between outlets of the same business. *Elastic demand* is where customers can choose from a range of outlets run by different operators – in towns there are many different pubs all offering similar products and styles, all in competition with each other for your custom.

Non-profit organizations

Are your prices market-driven or even commercial? They may be determined by some other factor, such as local authority regulations (such as school meals) or by union negotiation (as in a factory staff eating facility). As a result, even within the food-service sector, there may be different types of prices and hence different cost percentages. For contract catering, for example, prices may be low to keep the customers on-site for a short lunch break. The cost percentage may be very high as the company being serviced may pay for most of the additional costs such as payroll.

▶▶ ACTIVITY

How are prices determined in your organization? Are there different prices for the same product at different times? Are different methods used for different products? What about your meals, if you have them – how are they priced or costed?

Package pricing

We've looked at the different methods of pricing individual items and also quoting for a small group where only two elements are taken into account (room and breakfast) but you may also need to put together a single price which includes a range of items. The benefit of this to the customer is that they gain 'one-stop-shopping' – all the elements they need are grouped together in a single price and normally at a discount. For the operator there is also a benefit – only one price to charge the customer per item, not lots of separate charges, and so less cost in administration, stationery (for printing bills) and so on – and less likelihood of mistakes and queries.

Packages can be put together for all types of offers – a hotel weekend break, a conference centre package, a day trip to a theme park. They can be very low prices (food plus drink plus a disco, for instance) to enormously expensive such as a fully-inclusive round the world cruise.

The usual approach is to add the *selling prices* of all the different elements together and then apply some level of discount – but how much to give? Again this may depend on the time of year and how much you need the business to fill spare capacity (unused rooms, restaurant or airline seats are wasted if not used on the day – so any sale is better than none). At this point you can look at the *costs* for the different elements and, as long as they are all covered, you can quote a price somewhere between the cost price and the full selling price. The more you want the business, the more discount you are able to give.

Discounting package prices

There is a great deal more flexibility in a hotel or airline for changing package prices than there are in other sectors where the cost structures are different (see Chapter 4). Managers need to know that they cannot discount as much in a restaurant or tour package, for instance, as they can in a hotel or on a flight.

Here are two examples of a package – one for a conference in a hotel, the other a one-day tour to a city, including entrance to a museum. The prices for the individual items are the average prices charged to customers in the departments for these – for instance, breakfast is the normal menu price.

Conference		*One day Tour*	
Item	Price (£)	Item	Price (£)
Accommodation (2 nights)	160	Hire of coach	15
Breakfasts (2)	25	Driver	5
Buffet dinner	30	Courier/guide	5
Gala dinner	50	Entrance fees	5
Lunch (2)	40	Coffee break	5
Coffee/tea breaks (4)	10	Lunch	15
Meeting room hire	20		
Equipment hire	10		
Stationery/conference pack	5		
Total	350	Total	50

Which is the most flexible in terms of discounting? If you look back to the earlier chapters where we discussed profit margins you'll see that the accommodation area has the highest margins – and so the highest opportunity for discounts (hence the conference is more flexible on pricing).

▶▶ ACTIVITY

Look at a holiday brochure which allows a customer to put their own package price together (say a flight or ferry plus villa hire) and compare the prices for high season and low season. See if you can work out which are the most price-sensitive elements – that is, those that are discounted the most.

The need for information

This is crucial to the exercise! There's no point in trying to find the optimum price if you don't know all your costs. Managers need to have information about the market as well so that you know both 'sides' of the pricing argument – the accountant's and the marketer's information. This will ensure that you can make the best-informed decision which will (hopefully) satisfy the need for revenue and the need for profit (or covering the costs).

Breaking even

The last section of this chapter uses cost behaviour to work out how many of a product or service you need to sell in order to cover all your costs – in other words, to reach *break-even point* (BEP). After this point is reached then you can start to make a profit from all the extra items you sell.

To work out a BEP you need first to find the *Contribution margin* (CM). To do this you need to:

1   Split your costs into fixed and variable

2   Work out the total variable cost per customer or item sold

3   Find the price per customer or item

Then you can work out your CM. This takes the variable costs (those directly incurred by selling the item) and subtracts them from the selling price. It's usually expressed as a formula:

CM = SALES minus VARIABLE COSTS

The most common (and understandable) approach is to show it for a single unit.

Here's an example:

	(£)
Selling price	4.00
Variable costs	(1.60)
Contribution margin	2.40

Break-even point

Now you can work out the BEP. You could do this longhand but the simplest way is to use a formula. This takes the total fixed costs and divides them by the CM, preferably the CM per unit, so the formula is:

$$\text{Break-even point} = \frac{\text{Fixed costs}}{\text{Contribution margin/unit}}$$

This gives you the BEP in units, which is the point at which all costs have been paid for (fixed and variable).

Here's an example using the CM shown above. If the total fixed costs are £3,000 then the calculation is:

$$\text{Break-even point} = \frac{\text{Fixed costs}}{\text{Contribution margin/unit}} \quad \frac{£3,000}{£2.40} = 1,250 \text{ units}$$

To cover all the costs you need to sell 1,250 units at a selling price of £4.00 each. Alternatively, you can work out the total in sales revenue (money) and for this you use the contribution margin percentage, rather than the amount per unit.

The CM% for the above would be:

	(£)	(%)
Selling price	4.00	100.0
Variable costs	(1.60)	(40.0)
Contribution margin	2.40	60.0

Using the same BEP formula:

$$\text{Break-even point} = \frac{\text{Fixed costs}}{\text{CM \%}} \quad \frac{£3,000}{60.0\%} \quad = £5,000 \ (\text{revenue})$$

Check it back to see if it works – 1,250 units at £4 each equals £5,000 of sales.

BEP for profit

This process can also be used to calculate how many you need to sell to make a profit. What you do is add on the profit required to the fixed costs – and the rest of the formula is the same.

$$\text{Break-even point + profit} = \frac{\text{Fixed costs + Profit required}}{\text{Contribution margin/unit}}$$

Using the same CM and fixed costs as before, how many do you need to sell to make a profit of £600?

$$\text{Break-even point + profit} = \frac{\text{Fixed costs + Profit required}}{\text{Contribution margin/unit}} = \frac{£3,000 + £600}{£2.40} = 1,500 \text{units}$$

To prove the BEP + Profit works then you could check it back by calculating the P&L using 1,500 as the number of items sold.

	Total (£)	Per cover(£)	%
Sales revenue	6,000	4.00	100.0
Variable costs	(2,400)	(1.60)	(40.0)
Contribution margin	3,600	2.40	60.0
Fixed costs	(3,000)		
Profit	600		

Break-even charts

You could use a break-even chart to compare your pricing strategies. These line-charts are covered in the chapter on spreadsheets and charts. If you first plot the costs then you can plot the sales at different unit selling prices – say three different levels. Then you can find the BEP of each on the chart and compare them – and the profits. Here's an exercise to practise BEP:

London Restaurant Company

A restaurant company in London is planning to open a large new restaurant in an old warehouse open every day of the year. A return on investment of 15% (that is, profit) is required. The first year's budget is:

Average spend	£33.00
Cost of sales	32%
Other variable costs	15%
Salaries	£600,000
Rent and rates	£500,000
Insurance	£60,000
Depreciation	£400,000
Administration	£100,000

You are asked to calculate the number of covers per year:

a) for the restaurant to break even

b) for the restaurant to achieve the profit required

Here's the answer:

Fixed costs	(£)	Contribution margin	(%)	(£)
Salaries	600,000	Selling price	100	33.00
Rent and rates	500,000			
Insurance	60,000	Cost of sales	(32)	(10.56)
Administration	100,000	Other variable costs	(15)	(4.95)
Depreciation	400,000	= total variable costs	(47)	(15.51)
	1,660,000	CM %	53	17.49

a) Break-even point

$$\frac{\text{Fixed costs}}{\text{Contribution margin}} = \frac{£1,660,000}{£17.49} = 94,911 \text{ covers or 260 per day}$$

b) Profit required

Investment	£4,000,000
= profit required at 15%	£600,000

$$\frac{\text{Fixed costs} + \text{profit required}}{\text{Contribution margin}} = \frac{£2,260,000}{£17.49} = 129,217 \text{ covers or 354 per day}$$

This assumes that it is open every day of the year. What if it were not? Then the average per day would be different. You could try it for, say, 350 days.

And here's another exercise to practise both pricing and BEP together:

Farm park offer

A small farm park is looking to increase its number of visitors and revenues. One concern is that most groups typically bring their own packed lunch and so food sales are very low. The owners are considering offering a special rate to groups, which would include entrance to the farm park, a packed lunch and a small souvenir, for the months of June, July and August. The existing business gives the following results per month and will not be affected.

Visitors	6,500
Variable wages	£3,500
Variable expenses	£750
Variable overhead	£1,400
Fixed costs per year	£185,000
Profit % required	30%
Average entrance fee	£4.50

Anticipated costs for the special offer are the same except for initial promotion and advertising at £1,200 for the three-month season and an additional £2.50 variable costs for the lunch and souvenir.

Expected visitors are an average of 40 for each of the 8 weekend days each month, and 25 for each of the remaining days (weekdays).

Can you:

(a)   Work out the selling price per visitor for the package to achieve the required profit margin

(b)   Work out the number of visitors needed for the package to break even

(c)   Find the profit from the existing and new business.

TIP

The cost of the advertising needs to be split between all the estimated new visitors to find out the true gain from this extra business.

Here's the answer:

	June	July	August	Total
Total days	30	31	31	92
Weekend days	8	8	8	24
Visitors – weekend	320	320	320	960
Weekdays	22	23	23	68
Visitors – weekdays	550	575	575	1700
Total visitors	870	895	895	2660

Costs per visitor	Existing (£)	Extra (£)	New (£)
Variable wages	0.54		0.54
Variable expenses	0.12	2.50	2.62
Variable overhead	0.22		0.22
Total variable	0.88		3.38
Advertising (fixed)		0.45	0.45
= cost per visitor	0.88		3.83
Months in year	12		
Fixed costs per month	£15,417		
Months per season	3		
Visitors per season	19,500		

a) Selling price

Selling price equals	100%		
Profit % required	30%		
So the total cost % is	70%	which =	£3.83
Sales (gross up)	£3.83		
	70%	=	£5.46

b) Break even point

Contribution per unit

Selling price	£5.46		
Variable costs	-£3.38		
Contribution	£2.08		

BEP

Fixed costs	£1,200.00		
Contribution/unit	£2.08	=	575 visitors

c) Effect on profit

	Existing	New	Total	
Visitors (June-August)	19,500	2,660	22,160	
	(£)	(£)	(£)	(%)
Sales (Visitors x rate)	87,750	14,517	102,267	100.0
Variable costs	(16,950)	(8,962)	(25,912)	(25.3)
Contribution	70,800	5,555	76,355	74.7
Fixed costs	(46,250)	(1,200)	(47,450)	(46.4)
Profit	24,550	4,355	28,905	28.3

Summary

We've now reached the end of the fifth chapter that looked at pricing and break-even points. You have learned

▷   Different approaches to pricing – the accountant's methods and the marketers methods

▷   How to calculate a price from costs to achieve a standard gross profit

▷   How to calculate a price for a new project, based on the investment required

▷   The marketing approach to pricing

▷   What the relevance of contribution is to pricing

▷   How to calculate how many you need to sell to cover all your costs (break even point) and then to make a profit.

Quiz

1.   How do you gross up?

2.   What are the three main types of 'accountant's pricing'?

3.   What's the difference between price elasticity and price sensitivity?

4.   How do you find contribution – and what is it?

5.   What's the formula to calculate the BEP if you want to find the sales in money (not units)?

6

Forecasting

▼
▼
▼
▼
▼

Introduction

Within every business there's a need to plan ahead. If we didn't then there's a likelihood of not having enough food to cook, not enough staff to serve or lots of empty rooms. You could also have too many staff, or too much food, which would lead to wastage and unnecessary expense.

Forecasting is a simple technique that lets any manager plan for the more efficient working of their area, and use of resources. Generally forecasting means to 'look ahead' but in hospitality we use it to mean planning on a short-term basis – that is: tomorrow, next week, next month. The term 'budget' is used to mean a formal, detailed plan for the next financial year and 'strategic plan' for long-term (around five years) planning. We will look at these two briefly towards the end of this chapter but the main purpose is to look at forecasting and to see the effect of *not* planning ahead from both customer service and financial aspects. We'll also look at predicting cash flows, which helps the business manage their working capital.

By the end of this chapter, therefore, you will be able to:

▷   Understand the importance of forecasting to the business

▷   Calculate profits from forecasted volumes

▷   Differentiate between budgeting and strategic planning

▷   Calculate a cash forecast.

Why bother?

First of all let us consider the impact of *not* forecasting how many rooms in your guesthouse you will sell next Saturday night.

If you don't know how many guests you'll have:

▷   You won't be able to sell the empty rooms (losing revenue)

▷   You won't know how many sausages, or how much bread to order

▷   You won't know how many clean sheets and towels you will need

▷   You won't know how many staff to call in on Sunday morning to serve breakfast and clean the rooms.

Of course, you could order the same as you always do but that might cause wastage of food and have your staff standing around doing nothing – or run out of food and have the staff unhappy because they're overworked (and also unhappy customers who might not return).

Here's another example. If you run a theme park and don't forecast visitors for a Wednesday in autumn, term time, you could keep all your outlets open that would mean:

▷ Over-staffing

▷ Wasting food that doesn't get purchased and wasting electricity

▷ Upsetting customers because the food looks stale and the staff look unmotivated

▷ A loss of money as a result.

For cost sector and other types of catering (such as in hospitals and inflite catering) forecasting can be even more important as margins are so tight – if they don't forecast accurately there could be wastage which could mean the difference between break-even and a loss situation. So you can see that whatever the size and type of operation planning is important for everybody – and not just to save money.

What is forecasting?

Forecasting is usually a short-term prediction of levels of trade, which is more accurate than a budget that was probably prepared months ago. It's often more realistic – what we are likely to do rather than what we hope might happen. The approach tends to be more simple than a budget and may just be a prediction of volume (rooms, covers, visitors) to assist with staffing and ordering, or to identify gaps where an extra push on sales is required. So, a forecast allows planning of:

▷ Selling strategy

▷ Staffing (ratio of fixed headcount and casuals, or using up of holiday days)

▷ Maximization of occupancy and rate

▷ Open/closure policy for outlets

▷ Purchasing and storage (particularly perishable products)

▷ Cash flow.

How it works

Lets look at the process – Figure 6.1

Figure 6.1

Figure 6.1 is a forecast flow chart for a leisure hotel (the most complex type of structure).

The forecast starts with the yield management system which forecasts the rooms sold, and hence the sleepers (customers).

Rooms and sleepers information goes to:

▷ Reception and porters – for staffing levels at check in/out

▷ Housekeeping – for cleaning rooms and linen stocks

▷ Leisure (do they need golf lessons, beauty appointments?)

▷ Food and beverage

▷   Restaurants – for breakfast, lunch, dinner covers – and sales mix (and then to kitchen)

▷   Bars

▷   Conference and Banqueting

▷   Purchasing.

All these areas need to schedule staff, order goods, plan cleaning and set-up, and so on.

Lastly, all this information goes to:

▷ Financial Control – for planning cash flows and profit forecasts

Other sectors are, in theory, not so complex but may well be more difficult in practise. In hospitals, for instance, most of the cleaning is routine so not affected by volumes. Catering 'only' relies on staff numbers (probably fairly stable), visitors (probably similar) and patients. But – how do you predict the number of patients, and what they will be able to, or like to eat? Since food is important to recovery you would want to give patients food to tempt their appetite, but on a very limited budget you don't have scope for wastage. You will have to rely on experience, past trends and asking patients to order in advance.

So... we need to forecast

Daily — 'do we have spare tables we need to fill tonight?' 'Do I need an extra room attendant?' 'How many bread rolls should I order for tomorrow?'

Weekly — 'if next week's quiet we could use up some spare bank holidays that are owing'

Monthly — 'do we need to offer a discounted rate on our rooms next month?'

Seasonally — ' there's a new tourist bus running in the summer. Can I promote my attraction to these extra visitors?'

Why do we forecast?

– to enable managers to plan, and staff to work, more effectively.

Mini-case

A hotel chef considered himself to be an artist, not an accountant, so he ordered what he pleased. He couldn't be bothered with looking at forecasts of sleepers so he could estimate how many croissants he would need each morning – so he had a standard order.

Result:

▷   Some days there weren't enough croissants for the customers – equals unhappy customers

▷   Other days there were too many croissants so the staff had to eat Croissant Pudding (a version of bread-and-butter pudding) for lunch (again!) – equals unhappy staff.

Timing

Forecasting is done on a daily (perhaps by meal period), weekly or monthly basis particularly where business volumes are very changeable. If demand is stable and constant (residential care, long-stay hospitals, prisons, army catering) then you may think that forecasting isn't relevant. However, people have likes and dislikes and so you may still need to predict the menu-mix for ordering and production. You will see the effect if we look at a few examples.

A small visitor attraction

Next week's projected visitors

Day	Number
Monday	400
Tuesday	400
Wednesday	600
Thursday	800
Friday	1,200
Saturday	2,000
Sunday	2,200

Let's look at consumption. Forty percent will bring their own food (and sit in the picnic area, which will need cleaning). The rest will eat lunch in the outlets – half in the café, 10% in the restaurant and the rest from the takeaway (which also means mess in the picnic area). Half of all visitors will also eat ice creams (the weather is forecast to be very hot!).

Day	Number	Own food 40%	Eat lunch 60%	Café 50% of those eating lunch	Restaurant 10% eating lunch	Takeaway 40% eating lunch	Ice creams 50% total
Mon.	400	160	240	120	24	96	200
Tues.	400	160	240	120	24	96	200
Wed.	600	240	360	180	36	144	300
Thurs.	800	320	480	240	48	192	400
Fri.	1,200	480	720	360	72	288	600
Sat.	2,000	800	1,200	600	120	480	1,000
Sun.	2,200	880	1,320	660	132	528	1,100

In addition to the permanent staff, casual workers are needed. Extra staffing is based on one person per 200 visitors.

Day	Number	Casual staff
Mon.	400	2
Tues.	400	2
Wed.	600	3
Thurs.	800	4
Fri.	1,200	6
Sat.	2,000	10
Sun.	2,200	11

You now have predictions for both the catering outlets and staffing in terms of volume so you can plan your ordering. The same could be done for the shop although the number of items on sale will be greater, and they won't be perishable in the same way as food eaten on the day. It doesn't matter too much – unless it's nearing the end of the season – if you have too many postcards, key-rings and cuddly toys in stock.

In-flight catering

Flights for tomorrow (economy class only):

Destination	Paris	New York	Hong Kong
Snack	300		
Lunch		400	
Dinner			350
Breakfast			350

You normally allow 10% vegetarian who should have pre-ordered when their flight was booked, but don't always do so. Of the rest, the main meals are usually split equally between a meat and a fish dish (breakfast is split into meat or egg), to allow for dietary needs and taste. You also need to allow an extra 5% for staff food for the long-haul flights only (the Paris flight is so short the airline staff don't have time to stop for a break).

The Paris flight is easy – snacks are all the same and suitable for vegetarians, so the ordering and production planning is straightforward. The long-haul flights are a little more complex.

	New York	Hong Kong	
	Lunch	Dinner	Breakfast
	400	350	350
Add 5% staff	420	368	368
Vegetarian 10%	42	37	37
Meat 50% of the rest	189	166	166
Fish 50% rest	189	166	
Egg 50% rest			166

You would now need to add on the Club and first class passengers, who have different menus entirely.

Hotel staffing

A small hotel needs to consider how many staff it needs in addition to its core workforce. The action might be:

	Occupancy	Staffing
October	70%	1 extra required
November	80%	2 extra required
December	60%	Normal staff will cover
January	30%	Use up bank holidays and days owing

▶▶ **ACTIVITY**

Think of a fast-food outlet. What do they need to forecast? How would they use this to help plan staffing? Remember back to the flexible workforce approach and scheduling by the hour to match peaks and troughs in volumes.

Who does the forecast?

You do! If you are a manager in a unit or department then you know your business – and are the best person to estimate what's going to happen on a short-term basis. You may need information from other areas, but you should estimate realistically what the volumes are going to be.

▶▶ **ACTIVITY**

Does your department do any forecasting? If so, find out how it is done (if you're not directly involved) – what information is needed, and where this comes from. Why not then ask somebody else how their department or unit does it?

Forecasting profits

In addition to forecasting volumes, senior managers are also interested in forecasting sales and costs. This can be fairly simplistic, using (your) volumes, predicted average spends and the average costs per customer. Where you have fairly volatile segments then it helps to show the split of these too. This isn't just for accommodation – as we've seen other types of hospitality also have market segments. As an example, a casino can forecast different types of gamblers, by different types of day – these are 'graveyard', 'day' and 'swing' sessions (you can work out which is which!). They forecast:

▷ How many hours are played at each game

▷ How much is bet per game and per hour

▷ What the percentage of winnings is (to the gambler and to the house).

It works for both slot machines and table games and so gives data as to how much cash is needed too (there's more on cash flow later in this chapter).

Changes in levels of business

You can also use forecasting techniques to look at the effect of changes in levels of business. Here are some figures to calculate to see the effect of a 20% rise or fall in volume. (Yes, you can use cost volume profit – BEP-methods for this too.)

Guest house	Normal	Down 20%	Up 20%
Rooms sold	10		
Average rate	£30.00		
Breakfast cost per room	£2.00		
Staff and supplies cost per room	£5.00		
Revenue	£300		
Food cost	(£20)		
Staff and supplies	(£50)		
Fixed costs	(£60)		
Profit	£170		

TIP

Fill in the top sections (per person figures) first. The fixed costs and the costs per room don't change. Once you've got the new volumes then you can work out the totals.

Answer

	Normal	Down 20%	Up 20%
Rooms sold	10	8	12
	(£)	(£)	(£)
Average rate	30.00	30.00	30.00
Breakfast cost per room	2.00	2.00	2.00
Staff and supplies cost per room	5.00	5.00	5.00
Revenue	300	240	360
Food cost	(20)	(16)	(24)
Staff and supplies	(50)	(40)	(60)
Fixed costs	(60)	(60)	(60)
Profit	170	124	216

You can see the difference in profit for the different levels of business. These all look healthy but it might not have been so good on another day with different circumstances.

What if the costs are predicted to change too? What would happen if they all went up by 5%? Try this too – here's the grid again.

TIP

To add 5% multiply by 1.05. Do the per person figures first and then recalculate the totals.

	Normal	Down 20%	Up 20%
Rooms sold	10	8	12
Average rate	£30		
Breakfast cost per room	£2		
Staff and supplies cost per room	£5		
Revenue	£300		
Food cost	(£20)		
Staff and supplies	(£50)		
Fixed costs	(£60)		
Profit	£170		

The answer:

	Normal	Down 20%	Up 20%
Rooms sold	10	8	12
	(£)	(£)	(£)
Average rate	30.00	30.00	30.00
Breakfast cost per room	2.00	2.10	2.10
Staff and supplies cost per room	5.00	5.25	5.25
Fixed costs	60.00	63.00	63.00
Revenue	300	240	360
Food cost	(20)	(17)	(25)
Staff and supplies	(50)	(42)	(63)
Fixed costs	(60)	(63)	(63)
Profit	170	118	209

It doesn't look much for such a small business but imagine if it were 50 times bigger.

Here's a 'what if' question for you to practise.

Forecasted trade looks disappointing and the managers are trying to improve sales. They suggest that sales could be increased by 10% if they did a mailshot costing £500. The other possibility is spending £15,000 on new equipment that could also increase sales by £30,000. What should they do (ignore depreciation)?

Sales	£300,000
Food and Beverage costs	40%
Labour costs (variable)	20%
Salaries	10%
Other costs (variable)	8%
Fixed costs	20%

The answer:

	Original	Mailshot	Equipment
	(£)	(£)	(£)
Sales	300,000	30,000	30,000
F&B costs	(120,000)	(12,000)	(12,000)
Gross Profit	180,000	18,000	18,000
Less payroll (variable)	(60,000)	(6,000)	(6,000)
Less other variable costs	(24,000)	(2,400)	(2,400)
Contribution	96,000	9,600	9,600

Less fixed payroll	(30,000)		
Less other fixed costs	(60,000)		
Mailshot costs		(500)	
Equipment costs			(15,000)
Profit	6,000	9,100	(5,400)

You can see that either suggestion results in an extra £30,000 of sales and £9,600 of contribution. The problem is that the new sales incur additional costs. Yes – the mail-shot is worth it but (on paper) no, the equipment purchase isn't.

You do need to think long term about this, though. Will the mailshot generate a permanent increase in sales? Do you really need the new equipment anyway? It's never quite a simple as it looks!

▶▶ ACTIVITY

Can you see any areas in your work that could be improved by spending a small amount of money that would then either generate more sales or reduce costs? Why not put a few figures together. If they are beneficial, why not show them to your manager.

Formal forecasting methods

There are some complicated statistical (and graphical) methods of forecasting that are mentioned in many of the accounting textbooks. They use past data to plot trends and then forecast for the future. If you understand about regression and correlation then please read up about them – we don't cover them here.

Forecasting new products

Most of the forecasting we've discussed assumes that you've prior knowledge and lots of past data to help you. But what if you haven't? What if you have to plan from a 'zero-base'? It's then that you need a technique called Zero Based Budgeting (ZBB). If you read about it in some textbooks it can be described as a complex technique which requires looking at all aspects of an existing organization. In hospitality we tend to have our own definition, which is for new products.

It's also a 'bottom-up' approach and requires you to decide on every single aspect of your customers, their sales and costs. So, for a new hotel this can mean looking at every single market segment and guestimating how many rooms you will sell (each night), what the average room rate will be and so on. For costs you have to take every single type of cost and estimate how much you will use in the period. It can take a lot of time.

Mini-case

A hotel had been taken over and all past records removed. The new managers were upgrading the facilities and so decided to do a ZBB, with instructions to calculate *everything*. They decided they'd gone a bit too far with this when they realized somebody had spent an hour working out how many paperclips they might use in a month. The cost of this person's salary by far outweighed the benefit of this calculation – so she moved on to more important costs. Sometimes you can overdo things a bit!

Does it work?

ZBB is obviously based on a lot of guesswork, and market research. There are plenty of examples where it hasn't worked as well as it might have. Several well-known new projects have proved far less profitable than expected, because the visitor numbers just haven't achieved the levels that were estimated. Sometimes there's a political aspect to the project that means that it proceeds whereas if it were a commercial venture it might not.

Life span

Another factor that can influence the decision is the life of the project. If it's a one-off event that is budgeted then you also have to take the dismantling costs into account; again political considerations may outweigh the commercial aspects. There may also be a subsidy from another area that can counter-balance the losses on the hospitality section – and the four-yearly Olympics is a good example. There may be an overall loss on hospitality but this is balanced by the income from television rights and also the long-term gains to the local economy. ZBB techniques are used to calculate the costs, but the overall outcome (rather than just the financial output from hospitality) is what matters.

Budgets

Now a short explanation about budgets. If you want to read more about these then Peter Harris's book *Profit Planning* is a good place to start.

In hospitality a budget is a formal plan for the forthcoming financial year. It is mainly thought of as being financial but also considers how the business is performing now and what actions need to be taken to improve or maintain business levels. This could be a change of product or service, finding new markets, updating of technology and development of staff.

The types of budget are operational (like the departmental and front-page P&Ls), capital (all the new equipment and refurbishment required) and cash. They are combined into a 'master budget'.

So, they are needed:

▷   As a plan of action

▷   To set standards and establish responsibilities

▷   For reviewing current results

▷   To assist in evaluating trends.

Methods of budgeting

The budget planning process can take many months and requires input from a range of people and sources. There are two approaches – Top Down and Bottom Up.

Top down means that the owners decide how much money they want from their investment. They tell you what profits they expect (or the cost levels in a hospital for instance – top-down is common in the public sector). You then need to work your sales and cost to equal what's expected.

Bottom up means that the departments estimate what they can do and build up a budget from the estimated sales and costs, and then arrive at a profit. This approach involves all managers (and often supervisors too) so you may well be involved in the future. One of the benefits is that, by being involved, managers feel responsible for the figures that they have created and so are more likely to achieve them. This is part of responsibility accounting, which we mentioned in Chapter 2.

Not surprisingly there's often a mismatch between the 'bottom-line' figures of the two approaches, so there's often negotiation between the two 'sides' until a feasible budget is reached. This can take a lot of time.

Mini-case

The flagship property of a four-star hotel chain had spent several weeks preparing its budget in-house until the GM was happy. They took it to the Regional Director and after several changes (more revenue, less costs) and another two weeks, he was happy too. Then they took it to the Finance Director, and the same happened again. Eventually a budget was arrived at that everybody was reasonably happy with (though the GM was worried about his bonus) and the budget was 'put to bed'.

One week later the chain was put up for sale and they had to do a whole new budget which showed even more profit. Sometimes you just can't win.

How's it done?

The most common method is to use last year's figures as a basis and then build on from them, taking into account any changes in the market and the business that are likely to have an impact in the future. If you don't have past data then you need to 'zero-base' your budget, which we discussed earlier.

Don't forget too that you are restricted in what you can do – by the space you have available, the capabilities of staff, equipment available, money for capital expenditure and so on. These are called '*limiting factors*'. You can't build a new food outlet in your theme park if you don't have the space or the money, and you can't offer a new destination in your package holiday brochure if the accommodation and the flights are not available.

▶▶ ACTIVITY

Do you get involved in the budgeting process, or is it a top-down approach? Do you know what happens to the numbers after you do them? Ask your manager if you can talk through the budgeting process in your organization.

Strategic planning

This is long-term planning and often reviews five years ahead. Senior management looks at global and national trends and then makes decisions as to future business.

This may well affect you in the future if, for instance, they are going to expand (or contract) the business – so it's worth listening out for announcements as to future long-term plans. Expansion can mean more job opportunities whereas contraction might mean you have to do some strategic planning of your own as to when you need to find an alternative employer.

If you are thinking about opening your own business then you also need to plan strategically. When you discuss your ideas with a bank they are going to want to see:

▷   A three-year business plan. This isn't just the financial numbers (budget) but also how you are going to achieve it. Your marketing plans are as important as your financial plans. The bank wants to know how you will persuade customers to try your products, and how much they will spend. You will also need to plan your costs.

▷   Details of the fixed assets you need to buy, and the property if relevant

▷   A three year cash flow forecast (which we will do shortly).

So, strategic planning isn't just for 'top managers' – it affects you too.

Forecasting cash

We'll discuss the importance of cash as part of working capital as well as how to collect (and spend) it, in the next chapter. In this chapter we'll just look at how to predict cash levels at a particular time. This technique can be adapted to suit your own finances – in other words, to predict your own bank balance. First a reminder where cash comes from and goes to:

Cash in	Daily	Cash
		Cheques
		Credit cards (Access/Visa)
		Debit cards
	Monthly	Interest from banks and building societies
		Other investment income, rents and so on
Cash Out	Weekly	Payroll
	Monthly	Cheques to suppliers
		Payroll taxes
	Quarterly	Value Added Tax

So each month there are periods of high outgoings that can require large cash balances at the bank unless the business is careful to manage its cash.

How to calculate cash

Receipts   *less*   Payments   *equals*   Surplus or deficit for the month
   plus or minus   Opening cash balance   *equals*   Closing cash balance

But – we have to take into account the time people take to pay us and the time we take to pay our bills.

This is a simple cash flow exercise. Here are the first two months, please try to do the third month yourself. Each month consists of four weeks. To make it more straightforward we will assume that the business is just starting up and there haven't been any sales and costs before.

Sales	Month 1 = £3,000, month 2 = £3,600, month 3 = £4,000. 75% pay in cash, the rest by credit the following month
Cost of sales	40% of the sales, paid the following month ('in arrears')
Expenses	£700 per month, also paid in the following month
Payroll	30% of the sales figure, paid in the current month
Cash in the bank at the start ('opening cash')	£200

The best way to approach this is to do your 'workings out' before you try and plot when they will all be paid.

So, the process is:

1. Write down all the information you need

2. Do all the workings out

3. Draw up the table format, as below

4. Put the figures in the relevant spaces

5. Add up the totals and arrive at a bank balance (which should be the end figure on your bank statement)

Workings out

Month	1	2	3
	(£)	(£)	(£)
Sales	3,000	3,600	4,000
Cash 75%	2,250	2,700	
Credit 25%	750	900	
Cost of sales at 40% sales	1,200	1,400	

Expenses at £700/month	700	700	
Payroll at 30% of sales	900	1,080	
Opening cash balance	200		

Cash Forecast

Month	1	2	Outstanding
Receipts			
Cash	2,250	2,700	
Credit		750	900 Debtors (DR)
Total	2,250	3,450	
Payments			
Cost of sales		1,200	1,400 Creditors (CR)
Expenses		700	700 CR
Payroll	900	1,080	
Total	900	2,380	
Surplus/deficit for period	1,350	1,070	
Opening balance	200	1,550	
Balance carried forward	1,550	2,620	

The 'outstanding' column shows how much still has to be paid – £900 debtors (to come in) and £2,100 creditors (to go out) so the positive bank balance hides a lot of liability. Now it's your turn. These DRs and CRs need to be paid the following month so they've been put in the right places. You can use the spare column in the 'workings out' section above.

	1 (£)	2 (£)	3 (£)	Outstanding
Receipts				
Cash	2,250	2,700		
Credit		750	£900	DR
Total	2,250	3,450		
Payments				
Cost of sales		1,200	£1,400	CR
Expenses		700	£700	CR
Payroll	900	1,080		
Total	900	2,380		
Surplus/deficit for period	1,350	1,070		
Opening balance	200	1,550		
Balance carried forward	1,550	2,620		

If you had a minus figure to carry forward (a deficit) that shouldn't be a big problem if it's only for a month and you can see that you will be into surplus the next month. You just need to talk to your bank *before* you overdraw!

►► ACTIVITY

Look at your own personal cash flow and try to predict your cash coming in and going out for the next month. Then in a month's time see how accurate you were (and see if you've saved any money by being more conscious of what you were spending).

Lastly here's another forecasting exercise to try. A departmental budget has been established with the following standard percentages:

	(%)
Food and beverage costs	38.0
Wages (variable)	19.5
Salaries	9.0
Fixed costs	20.0
Variable expenses	4.5
Net Profit	9.0
= Total sales	100.0

After several months of trading it is apparent that the sales will only achieve a figure of £300,000, a shortfall of 20% on the budget. A forecast is required to predict the anticipated net profit, in order that remedial action may be taken where necessary.

TIP

Work out the budget sales first, and gross up, then you can work out the budget costs. Remember that fixed costs don't change – and some of those above are fixed. Once you've got the budget for them, they will stay the same amounts for the forecast.

Answer

Workings out					
Forecast sales	£300,000				
Shortfall	20.0%				
Therefore forecast =	80.0% (of budget)				
Budget	£375,000				

		Budget	Forecast	Variance	Variance
	(%)	(£)	(£)	(£)	(%)
Total sales	100.0	375,000	300,000	75,000	20.0
Food and beverage costs	(38.0)	(142,500)	(114,000)	(28,500)	20.0

Wages (variable)	(19.5)	(73,125)	(58,500)	(14,625)	20.0
Variable expenses	(4.5)	(16,875)	(13,500)	(3,375)	20.0
Contribution	38.0	142,500	114,000	28,500	20.0
Salaries	(9.0)	(33,750)	(33,750)	0	0.0
Fixed costs	(20.0)	(75,000)	(75,000)	0	0.0
Net Profit	9.0	33,750	5,250	28,500	84.4

Hence the result is NOT a 20% drop in profits – but an 84% shortfall. This is because the fixed costs still stay the same. Variable costs have dropped in line with sales but there is still this large chunk of costs that has to be paid for. If this were your situation you would have to see if you could do anything about the sales, but also anything about the fixed costs.

Summary

You have now finished chapter 6. In this chapter we considered the importance of forecasting and why it matters to business. We also looked at cash and at the difference between strategic planning, budgeting and forecasting. You have, therefore:

▷　Considered the importance of short-term planning within the business

▷　Seen what a difference a forecasted shortfall or overage can make to your profits

▷　Calculated variances due to shortfalls in business volumes

▷　Discussed the different types of business planning – forecasting, budgeting and strategic planning

▷　Identified area where zero-based budgeting might be used

▷　Calculated cash balances.

Quiz

1. What's a forecast?

2. Who does it?

3. What's a budget?

4. What's a cash forecast?

5. Is a deficit on the month a problem?

6. Why bother with the outstanding column?

7

Managing cash and stocks

▼
▼
▼
▼

Cash ◄

Bank accounts ◄

Credit settlement ◄

Stock management ◄

Introduction

This chapter considers the two main physical items that have potential for control problems – cash and stocks. They are part of what's known as the cycle of working capital. We've seen in earlier chapters some of the ways in which these can be managed effectively but we will now concentrate on specific areas for control. First we will look at cash being both received and paid. Second, we will consider the flow of stock and the various stages at which problems can occur.

By the end of this chapter you will, therefore, be able to:

▷   Describe the cycle of working capital

▷   Identify the various stages at which cash moves in and out of the business

▷   Identify the various stages through which stock moves around the business

▷   Discuss methods of control appropriate to the operation

▷   Calculate ratios relevant to cash and stock control.

Cash

Cash is the 'lifeblood' of the business – without it you can't pay the bills or your staff and hence businesses can fail if they don't have enough of it. Here we will show you where the cash comes from and goes to, and how you can improve the cash flow of your business. You should note that cash is NOT the same as profits – businesses can be profitable but fail due to inadequate cash flow. We looked at forecasting cash flow in Chapter 6.

Working capital

Cash is part of working capital, which we know from Chapter 2 is the money to run the business. As a reminder it's worked out by taking:

Current assets (CA = cash, stock, debtors, prepayments) LESS
Current liabilities (CL = accruals, overdrafts, creditors).

Generally speaking, if there are more CA than CL then the business is 'liquid' which means able to pay its debts. There are two ratios that are used to express this – the Current ratio and Liquidity Ratio (also called the acid test).

Current ratio $\quad = \quad \dfrac{\text{Current assets}}{\text{Current liabilities}}$

This is expressed as a x : 1 – the CL being the 1. So, if you have £200 of CA and £100 of CL then the ratio is expressed as 2 : 1.

But stocks take a long time to convert into cash (they have to be converted to products, then sold and the cash collected) and so they aren't as 'liquid' as the other CA. It's best if they are extracted before you make the comparison – if the CA without the stock is more than the CL then you're OK.

Liquidity ratio
(Acid Test) $\quad = \quad \dfrac{\text{Current assets minus stock}}{\text{Current liabilities}}$

The 'acid test' is whether the liquidity ratio is better than 1.1 : 1 (as in £110 : £100). If it is then you have enough surplus of CA (without the stock) over CL to comfortably pay your bills. Even if the liquidity ratio is less than 1:1 then (although technically insolvent) it's not a disaster – you can usually borrow money – assuming that it is only a short-term problem and not a long-term shortage of money.

We need to understand how money moves around the business so that we can see where it comes from and goes to. This is the 'cycle of working capital'.

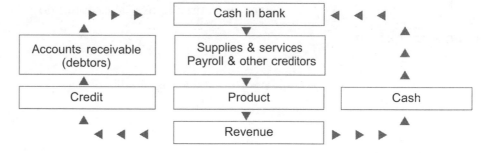

Figure 7.1 Cycle of working capital

1. First, cash is in the bank (or floats)

2. Then it gets paid out to food and beverage and other suppliers, government agencies, utility companies (all 'accounts payable' or 'creditors'), staff (as payroll) and so on – this takes time

3. The purchase of these produces a product or service, which is sold to give revenue

4. The revenue is paid for – either by cash or credit

5. Cash sales go directly back to the bank

6. Credit sales (debtors or 'accounts receivable') have to be collected (which takes time as well) until eventually they are paid which also becomes cash in the bank.

Now lets look at the different elements (excluding accruals and prepayments which we covered in Chapter 2). As with other aspects of control there are two potential problems – fraud (deliberate – and cash is very attractive) and errors (not deliberate and more to do with inefficiency).

Physical Cash

This comes into the operation in three ways:

Cash from customers

▷ Sterling cash

▷ Foreign exchange

▷ Credit cards (Access, Visa, etc.)

▷ Debit cards

▷ Cheques

▷ Vouchers (these aren't physical cash but do have a value

Cash from debtors

▷ Cheques

▷ Bank transfers (including credit cards)

This can also include advance deposit payments for future bookings

Cash from interest and commission

▷ Bank and building society interest

▷ Commission on foreign exchange

Cash should be stored in three places – the till, the safe or the bank – but of course it's not that simple, which is where the problems are likely to appear. Money has to be moved from place to place.

Customer	→	waiting staff (or receptionist, for instance)
Waiting staff	→	cashier
Cashier	→	cash office
Cash office	→	bank

Cheques received from debtors are received by post, ideally by a secretary or administrative assistant so that the potential for fraud is reduced.

| Secretary | → | cash office (or perhaps via a PMS – property-management system) |
| Cash office | → | 10 bank |

All these stages have potential for error or fraud although the opposite argument is that the more checks that are made the less likelihood there is for problems. Let's consider the different types of problems that can occur with cash.

Floats

Floats can be small (say £20 for each of the bar staff) or enormous (£1,000 for a hotel cashier who has to make a lot of foreign exchange transactions). The usual approach is that the float is always kept at exactly the same level, and any other cash received is banked whether it is correct or not. Each member of staff is responsible during their shift for their own float but when they go off duty it is either checked and signed over to a new member or staff or is put in the safe. If the business closes for the night then all floats should be kept in the safe – staff should never be allowed to take cash off the premises.

▶▶ **ACTIVITY**

How safe are your floats, if you have them? Look carefully at the procedures for opening and closing safes, tills and floats. Are tills left open at night so they are obviously empty? Do two people always open the safe, and two check the cash to make sure there is no theft? Do you feel secure yourself when handling cash, or could security be improved?

Cash moving around

This can also offer opportunity for thieves so, if possible, two people should always go together – whether it's paying in to a cash office or emptying telephone boxes or vending machines. It's both protection from attackers and a witness to correct procedures in case of suspicion.

Mini-case

Joe was responsible for 'cashing up' at the end of the night on his own. He had to lock the takings and floats in the safe and then leave the keys in a sealed envelope ready for collection by the early duty manager.

One morning the manager came on duty, opened the safe – but it was empty. Joe did not come to work that afternoon, and was never seen again. The police found out he had gone back to his home country where he could not be prosecuted.

From then on the manager ensured that the cashing up and closure of the safe was witnessed, and signed for, by two people. They could still have colluded in a fraud, but this was far less likely now.

Cash office

Bigger businesses often have a cash office (or part of a manager's office) where the main safe is kept holding larger floats with change and petty cash. These need to be very secure both outside (lots of locks, ideally with a combination code that is changed weekly) and inside – two separate keys and a combination code. It's also sensible not to allow more than one or two staff to enter the office at any one time.

Some busy cash offices operate like banks with security windows through which the transactions are made. They may also have a night safe facility so late working staff can deposit their takings when the cash office is closed. Security cameras are useful too.

Customers paying cash

In restaurants, making staff responsible for collecting payments from customers is one of the best incentives for accuracy, especially if they are subject to disciplinary action if they lose money. Some businesses deduct shortages from pay, but others argue that this is demotivating and just not practical. Whatever the approach, you need to have a written policy that anybody who has more than (for instance) 3 errors in a particular time span has to be retrained, which may mean they suffer a lower pay rate until they have proved that they are capable again.

Walk-outs

It can be a problem stopping 'walk-outs' – if customers want to leave without paying then they will usually find a way somehow. This is theft, though, which eventually affects the business as a whole and so threatens your jobs. Many times you can take payment in advance (in a hotel, for a wedding reception, a theatre outing or a holiday) but this isn't feasible for an ordinary meal. All you can do is to be vigilant and try and stop people walking out. Attitudes can vary – after all, you expect to pay on arrival to go to the cinema so why should customers object if asked to pay for a hotel room before they enter it?

Foreign exchange

Most EPOS and PMS systems can now be programmed to accept the major currencies so it will work out the rate for you. You do need to watch out for forged notes though (as you do with sterling) as it can be easy to 'pass off' forgeries if you are unfamiliar with a particular currency. The exchange rate you give appears worse than the bank rate as it includes the cost of commission that the business has to pay.

Accepting cheques

If possible – don't! And certainly don't cash them for money, only accept them in payment of goods. Most people now have credit or charge cards, which are safer (more about these later on). If you must accept them then you need to also see the customer's cheque card which will guarantee the cheque up to a certain amount (it's printed on the card). You should write the details from that on to the back of the cheque (and probably swipe it through the EPOS too). Some guarantee cards now have a photo of the owner on them, so it's worth looking out for that as well. Don't forget to check that the signatures are the same too, please!

Credit and debit cards

Wherever possible, encourage the use of credit cards (Access and Visa) or debit cards rather than charge cards, as they are cheaper and safer. The cashier swipes the card through the PDQ ('Pretty Damn Quick' – yes, it does mean that!) machine and then keys in the amount of money. Not only does the system (via telephone lines back to a central computer) check that the card isn't stolen or the customer exceeded their spending limit but also it then pays the cash from the operator (Access or Visa) into your bank account in the next few days.

If you don't have a PDQ then you will have to use a manual imprint machine and make sure that you check all the details. The card companies send out information to every business about what to check for – so make sure that you are doing this correctly. Again, don't forget to see that the signatures and amounts tally.

▶▶ **ACTIVITY** ━━━━━━━━━━━━━━━━━━━━━━

Think about the last few times you've paid in a shop or restaurant with a credit card. Did they check your signature or just hand the card back to you. What if that hadn't been your card but somebody else's – would they have noticed? It's frightening how easy it is to use a card, isn't it? Credit card fraud is ENORMOUS, whether from theft of cards or by 'skimming' which is making a copy of a card and then buying items on somebody else's account.

Bank accounts

There are many different types of accounts available and it isn't part of this book to explore these. The main advice for the small business is to:

▷ Discuss terms – after all, they are borrowing *your* money

▷ Use current and deposit accounts, and make sure you keep the business money separate from personal money. It's also worth while keeping all the tax you have to pay (PAYE and VAT) in a separate account so you aren't tempted to use it

▷ If you have a temporary cash shortage then it may be cheaper to overdraw for one day rather than taking money out of a high-interest-bearing account.

Banking

Banking deposit slips need to be filled in by one person and ideally checked by another, unless it's your own business.

Do you bank daily? Does someone actually go to the bank or do you have a security company to collect it? Security aspects should be paramount for both cash and staff – and your costs may be partly offset by savings on insurance premiums.

If you do visit the bank then you should change the time and route you take as even small amounts of cash can be tempting to thieves (it only takes a few snatches of a couple of thousand each to build up to a nice holiday fund).

Reconciling cash

Once banked you need to reconcile the amounts to the revenue figures. There's actually a three-way check:

Cash recorded via EPOS or PMS → Cash received by staff → Cash banked.

Once the bank statement is received then you need to check that too. Ideally they all tally – if they don't, then you need to see where the differences are and who is responsible for the shortage or overage.

Mini-case

One accounts clerk at head office reconciled all the bank statements of a company. He was a very conscientious worker, rarely took holiday and insisted that (if he were away) nobody else should do his job – he would catch up when he returned. All seemed fine until one day he was suddenly taken seriously ill.

Senior managers appointed a replacement clerk who found that money had been siphoned out of bank statements into the accounts clerk's own account where they earned a vast amount of interest. A couple of months later the money was returned so that the old accounts could be balanced.

If more than one person had checked the statements then this should not have happened.

Credit settlement

Types of credit settlement are credit account (account to company or travel agent voucher) or charge card (American Express, Diners and similar). The same processes apply as with credit cards (above) except that it may take a bit longer to gain payment. Another type of short-term credit is hotel guests signing items to their room accounts. Here it's important that staff are trained to check key cards, for signatures as well as room numbers, to ensure that the charge is made to the correct account.

Credit accounts

'Credit is a privilege not a right'

There is often a conflict between:

Sales staff (rooms, meals, conferences, etc.) who see success in terms of customers	Versus	Credit control staff who see success in terms of cash in the bank

Effective collection is dependent upon:

Before the event

▷ Applicants for credit being fully vetted (you can do this on-line now, in minutes) with full credit and bank references

▷ Agreements being signed with strict credit terms

▷ Staff who take bookings being trained not to give credit without authority.

At the event

▷ Correct and legible billing (prices, number of customers) and correct documentation (vouchers, correspondence)

▷ Organizer signing off to approve bill before departure.

Invoicing

▷ Details being checked again

▷ Correct name and full address (it's surprising how many invoices can get 'lost' within a company if the exact recipient isn't specified)

▷ Timely mailing of invoices.

Collection of debts

▷ Timely mailing of statements

▷ Resolution of queries

▷ Frequent and effective collection calls

▷ Paying in of cheques as soon as they arrive

▷ Encouraging direct transfers (see paying bills, below)

▷ Motivation of staff (incentives?)

▷ Commitment of *all* management (not just Financial Control).

Sanctions if they don't pay

▷ Use Sales and Marketing departments to pressure large producers

▷ Make use of any mutual contacts

▷ Threaten withdrawal of business

▷ If all else fails, don't be afraid to use professional help – a solicitor's letter can work very quickly. You can also use the Small Claims Court cheaply and efficiently to recover debts.

Measuring debtors

You can just use the 'debtors' figure on the BS but the main measure is 'debtor days'.

$$\text{Debtor Days} \quad = \quad \frac{\text{Average debtors}}{\text{Average daily credit sales}} \quad = \quad \text{days}$$

As an example, take the debtors figure as £5,000 and the credit sales for a month (30 days) £3,750 then the calculation would be:

$$\text{Average daily credit sales} \quad = \quad \frac{\text{Sales for month}}{\text{Number of days}} \quad = \quad \frac{£3,750}{30} \quad = \quad £125 \text{ per day}$$

$$\text{Debtor days} \quad = \quad \frac{\text{Debtors}}{\text{Average daily credit sales}} \quad = \quad \frac{£5,000}{£125} \quad = \quad 40 \text{ days}$$

That means that, on average, customers are taking nearly 6 weeks to pay the credit bills to you. Since some will pay quickly (perhaps in 2 weeks) – some are taking much longer. Forty days is manageable but it would help your bank balance if you could reduce this to a 30-day average.

Paying bills (creditors)

Payments are made to employees, suppliers for goods and services, statutory bodies (tax, VAT and so on) and local shops via petty cash.

Employees

Staff may be paid weekly or monthly (occasionally fortnightly) and you can't delay this as it will *immediately* affect morale and hence all aspects of the business. Some staff may still be paid in cash but most (including casual staff) are now paid through BACS (Bank Automated Clearing System) which transfers the money at a given time from your account to theirs.

Suppliers

These are paid on a regular basis that is usually monthly although sometimes you may agree specific short payment terms in exchange for cheaper prices. Services (utilities, telephone) often specify payment within two or three weeks.

Statutory bodies

VAT and tax authorities have fixed payment terms that you can't afford to ignore as the fines can be **very** large and are rigidly enforced. They may also close you down if you persistently default on payments (and in the event of liquidation they claim their cash before anybody else).

Petty cash

This is a small float kept in the business for you to use in emergencies or where it's not worth ordering from a supplier. For instance, if you only want to buy one packet of envelopes then it will be easier (and perhaps cheaper) to nip to the local stationers, rather than placing an order.

Helping cash flow

▷ Hold back supplier cheques as long as possible BUT don't jeopardise goodwill or future deliveries.

▷ Delay tax payments until the last possible date and use BACS or CHAPS (similar to BACS).

▷ See whether it's worth taking the discounts offered by suppliers for quick payment.

AND don't use that old favourite 'the cheque's in the mail' too often!

E-pay

We've already mentioned BACS which has been available for many years now. The trend is for fully automated electronic payments – or 'e-pay'. It's part of the entire business-to-business (B2B) and business-to-customer (B2C) revolution that's taking place – and by the time you read this it will already have moved on further. E-pay allows links between customer, business and bank. Simply stated it works like this:

1. You approve a supplier invoice for payment on your computer

2. Your computer tells the bank computer to pay £X on a specific date

3. The bank computer pays the cash from your bank account to the supplier bank account

4. It then tells the supplier and your computer that this has happened.

Measuring how long it takes to pay your bills

We use a similar calculation to debtors – this time it's creditor days.

$$\text{Creditor Days} = \frac{\text{Average creditors}}{\text{Average daily purchases}} = \text{days}$$

An example, take the purchases for 30 days are £15,000 and the creditor figure is £27,500.

$$\text{Average daily credit purchases} = \frac{\text{Purchases for month}}{\text{Number of days}} = \frac{£15,000}{30} = £500 \text{ per day}$$

$$\text{Creditor days} = \frac{\text{Creditors}}{\text{Average daily purchases}} = \frac{£27,500}{£500} = 55 \text{ days}$$

Your suppliers are probably NOT very happy at waiting so long for payment. You need to take some action or they'll refuse to do business with you!

Mini-case

A tourist hotel was owned (and lived-in) by a gentleman who hated paying bills. Unfortunately he also insisted on signing all cheques himself.

The telecom company arrived to cut off the telephones due to non-payment of the invoice. It was only by the financial controller telling the owner he wouldn't be able to call his friends (this was before mobile phones) that the cheque was signed.

Stock management

We have mentioned stock control before as being closely linked to cost control and to standard costing. Here we will be looking at the processes involved in the conversion of a raw material to an item for sale – ordering, delivery, storage and issue to departments. There is more about production and usage in the standard costing (Chapter 8) and ratios were discussed in Chapter 4 on cost control. The processes are particularly designed for food and beverage although there is application for any other items that are ordered by the unit. Figure 7.2 is a flow chart of the processes.

Figure 7.2 Stock flow chart

A couple of overall points about stock control. First, you need to set up systems that are safe and secure so the potential for fraud or wastage is limited. Second, you can't do everything, so you need to minimize the opportunities. If you don't spot problems early, whatever they are, then they will just get worse. In hospitality, too, you can have hundreds of stock items that aren't used very often and these are not really worth spending too much time on. It's the big things you really need to concentrate on.

Stock Items

Let's look at the type of stock items you find in hospitality and tourism. They are generally divided into two categories, perishable and non-perishable.

Perishable

These are mainly food-stuffs but some beverage has a short life-span too. They need to have a fast turnover in order to maintain their quality. Low levels of stock are possible with daily deliveries, which is usual in large cities but may be less common in rural areas.

You need to keep minimum stocks so that freshness is maintained, but without compromising on customer service. Some sectors have converted to longer-life products (packaged or frozen) to reduce loss and help with portion control.

Non-perishable

These tend to have larger holdings as deliveries are generally less frequent.

Liquor may have a large number of stock items, depending on the type of operation and the length of the wine list. It's often valuable and hence desirable to would-be thieves.

Supplies includes a range of departmental and administrative expenses – guest supplies, paper goods, cleaning materials, printed items.

Plant includes china, glass and cutlery and sometimes repairs and maintenance items.

Purchasing

Suppliers

One of the best ways of reducing the cost of what you buy is to 'shop around' for discounts on what you buy. This isn't possible for everybody, though, because you may be 'tied' into buying from nominated suppliers, such as beverage from the brewery. Larger organizations (hospital trust, contract caterers, hotel and leisure groups) almost always have a head office purchasing department, which can negotiate discounted prices from approved suppliers, which may be the difference of profit or loss on a contract.

If you are a small local business you can choose your suppliers and there may be strong arguments for buying from other local traders. They may not be the cheapest but they should give you good service and be able to supply you at short notice if you need it. You could buy fresh produce locally but go to a 'cash and carry' warehouse to buy all your dry goods, cleaning materials and so on. For beer you can negotiate with a range of breweries and perhaps obtain discounts of up to 20% on the prices a tied house might have to pay.

Specification

It is essential to ensure that you buy the right product for the right purpose or your costs will be incorrect. This applies whether you are buying china, meat, cleaning products or new beds. You need to research what you need for the job and then ideally produce a product specification that details everything you need. For a bunch of bananas this could include: size, number per bunch (yield), ripeness, packaging, preservatives, country of origin, colour, date and time of supply as well as cost.

Large businesses such as contract caterers have very strong specifications. They will negotiate lower prices in return for guaranteed volume of supply, which benefits both supplier and caterer. Smaller businesses may find it more effective to shop around for goods, although you may consider that you are better using your energies serving your customers.

Orders

For day-to-day purchases, managers normally have authority to buy what they need, providing they are documented and that it's obvious they are not for the manager's personal consumption. Standard orders may be pre-printed or on a computer system.

For bigger, occasional purchases, (unless you're a small business) you will need to complete a purchase order which will then have to be approved by senior management – and the level of authority often depends on the value of the goods. You normally should have three quotations from different suppliers to show that you have 'shopped around' for the best price.

How much to order

Order what you need! This may seem simple but many businesses just guess (remember the croissant pudding example quoted earlier). This means:

1.   Looking at your stocks to see how much you have

2.   Doing a forecast of what you will need until the next delivery

3.   Adding a bit more 'just in case'

4.   And then placing the order.

Even if you 'batch cook', say in a food production unit, the same principles apply. There's no point in ordering things you don't need because you then have problems of storage and deterioration (and you spend cash that could be better in the bank). This is one reason why ordering from a supplier is better than going to a cash-and-carry as you are less tempted to buy more.

▶▶ **ACTIVITY**

Think about the last time you went to a supermarket. Did you just buy what was on your shopping list, or did you add things you didn't really need? You probably do the same if you buy for work. Shopping lists are useful in business too, especially if you stick to them.

The other temptation is discounts. How many establishments have items on their shelves that they bought as there was a special offer – and never used?

Mini-case

A business was made an 'offer it couldn't refuse' – two cases (24 bottles in total) of what was then *the* fashionable summer drink for cocktails at a 50% discount. The problem was that fashions change. Two years later they finally realized that only 3 bottles had been used and 21 bottles were still in the cellar gathering dust. Eventually they were given to charity for raffle prizes.

There is a formula approach to ordering called the 'economic order quantity' – read it up in textbooks if you want to (see the list at the end of the Chapter). It's OK if you're in a manufacturing environment (which some catering businesses obviously are) but it's a bit cumbersome for day-to-day use.

Systems

There are lots of computerized stock control systems available now which will often also produce orders for you. It takes the stock levels held (about which more below), you add your forecast information and then it produces an order. Sometimes, with very sophisticated systems, the computer will even e-mail the order through to the supplier for you. This is good in theory and works well for dry goods but is less successful when dealing with some fresh food. Perhaps today you want a larger size steak or melon than yesterday, for a specific dish – it's not always easy to tell a pre-programmed computer this and persuade it to order what you want.

Remember, if one person orders all your stocks that could mean they have responsibility for millions of pounds of items. So, it's essential to:

▷   Have somebody of high enough calibre to do the job

▷   Accurately forecast need

▷   Negotiate contract prices and specifications if feasible

▷   Change suppliers if their service declines or they become too expensive

▷   Ensure managers know how much things cost

▷   Take advantages of discounts and rebates

▷   Minimize 'kickbacks' and freebies' – you'll end up paying somehow.

Receiving

This activity is really important! The 'back door' is traditionally one of the major places where losses can occur, usually due to fraud but occasionally just carelessness. Again it's crucial to have somebody you can trust to be vigilant, honest and accurate to receive goods – if you can't do it yourself. Think of the thousands of pounds worth of stock that is delivered every year, and wonder why the goods receiving clerk (if there is one) is paid so little.

The overall process is that you:

1.   Arrange deliveries at suitable times (you don't want four at once)

2. Check everything physically and compare it to what is written on the delivery note and on your copy of the order form. Write any discrepancies on the delivery note

3. Ttake responsibility for the goods and then move them to a safe place

4. Date stamp (and perhaps bar-code if you have a computerized system) everything to ensure correct stock rotation

5. Make sure the driver doesn't have access to other stock

6. Enter all deliveries on the computer system (if you have one), by item and price, which will update the stock records and help calculate costs.

The checking process depends on the type of goods that are being received.

Cleaning materials: Check brand name, size, quantity and perhaps strength

Stationery: Check items, number, colour if relevant

Paper goods: Check quantity, printed logo if ordered, type

Dry goods (food): Check type, size, quantity and that containers are sealed

Frozen food: Should be delivered in a special vehicle. Check type, size, quantity and temperature, and move immediately to freezers

Fruit and vegetables: Check all items per the standard specification – this could be all the items mentioned above for bananas. Otherwise it's size, number, ripeness, and overall quality

Meat and fish: These need really careful checking. You must check the cut, weight (per portion and total), quality, freshness, temperature. They should be delivered in refrigerated vehicles but not be frozen (they can contain a lot of water if they are) unless that's what you've ordered

Beer kegs: Check kegs are full and have correct beer type on label and that dates are correct. Chalk them to show receipt. Check empty kegs out and hand over to drayman

Bottled beer and soft drinks: Check all crates are full and bottles are sealed. Check out counted empties, in crates, to drayman

Tanked beer or postmix: These are delivered by 'tanker' and will be pumped directly into your storage containers. Check the meter before and after the delivery. The quantity delivered then needs checking against the meters on the tanker to make sure they match.

Wines and spirits: Check by name, type, size, quantity and that containers are sealed. You may put coloured labels on to show they are legitimate stock.

Suppliers don't usually take away empties (use a bottle bank instead) but if they do, check them out too.

Some items may be delivered directly to a unit – either by the delivery person or by the receiving clerk. Fresh produce often bypasses stores and goes straight to a kitchen. If this happens then the same processes need to take place.

▶▶ **ACTIVITY**

How are things received in your operation? Are the controls watertight or do you think that some items are 'going walkabout'? If so, is there anything you can do about this?

Storage

You need to keep stock safely and securely so that it doesn't 'walk' or deteriorate. You also need to make sure that it is consumed before its 'use by' date, so stock rotation is very important.

Legal requirements

There is a lot of health and safety legislation about storing different types of products. Many need storing separately (meat separate from fish, cleaning materials apart from food, and so on) so you must check that you are following correct procedures. If you need help on this contact your local council or your professional association (see the Web-site list at the back of the book). You also need a food hygiene certificate if handling food, and other certified training if you're handling certain chemicals or gas.

Rotation

Stock rotation generally follows the FIFO rule – 'first in first out'. This can be tricky if you're not organized in your stores, freezers or fridges. The rules are:

▷   Date stamp everything if it doesn't already have one

▷   Move old stock to the front and new stock to the back

▷   Periodically check that the stock is being used. If it isn't then you need to take action. This could mean putting on a special promotion to sell it off cheaply, asking the chef to use it up in staff meals or contacting the supplier to see if it can be returned. If you can't use it then see if a charity can take it from you. You'll have to 'write off' the value (which means it becomes a cost to the business) but at least it's not then taking up space and potentially going off

▷   If stock does deteriorate then it needs disposing of – again there are rules, and about chemicals in particular.

Keeping stock safe can be as simple as a good lock and only two keys (one in use and one in the safe as a spare). If you have to have more keys then they need to be signed in and out so that you always know who has access and therefore who is responsible. All the sophisticated stock systems in the world are useless if somebody can walk in and take things.

You may have many storage areas – the more outlets you have the more stores you'll have. Managers like to have their stock accessible, which helps them supply customers but can be a problem for control. Ideally you have a main stores area and then keep minimum stocks in departments.

Mini-case

Jim was a chef. He worked long hours and was a trusted member of the team. Just after he had left the premises late one evening he returned, escorted by a policeman. Jim had tripped on the pavement (perhaps having imbibed some of the kitchen brandy, but that's another story) and the policeman heard a 'clink' of metal and decided to investigate further. Not only was Jim 'borrowing' some of the cutlery belonging to the business (he was having a dinner party the following day) but he had also walked out with several kilos of prime steak.

Stock levels

For fresh food, stock levels often depend on demand – and that depends on accurate forecasting. Depending on the availability of deliveries you really only want a couple of days worth of fresh food in your fridges and stores so you plan the ordering so minimum stocks are held. You can usually buy in fairly small quantities to match what you need.

For dry and frozen goods you often have to order by case and also might only be able to get a delivery once a week or so, so stocks can fluctuate a little. You may want to keep about two weeks supply of these, on average. For keg and bottled beer (which can go off quite quickly) a low stock level is also advisable. Wines and spirits can usually be ordered in single bottles.

It obviously depends on location as to the availability of supply. If you're on a remote island and the boat comes once a week then you may have to have higher stock levels and different menus than if you were in the middle of the city. Cruise ships also have to keep high stock levels due to problems of supply, and negotiate for fresh food in a variety of locations.

Mini-case

A purchasing manager heard 'on the grapevine' that the price of coffee from South America was likely to rise substantially due to a bad crop, and so ordered several months' supply. He forgot that there are other areas in the world that also grow coffee. These had an excellent harvest and, as a result, the price of coffee actually went down. The result was that the business paid more for coffee overall than it needed to, this took an enormous amount of storage space and cash was used for buying this which could have been invested.

Par stocks

For many items you need to establish a *par* stock – a level of stock that is high enough to keep you supplied but low enough not to tie up space or cash.

How to calculate a par level:

1. Find out how often you can receive a delivery (say every seven days)
2. Add on the number of days between ordering and delivery (say another two)
3. Work out how many you consume in this number of days (nine in total)
4. Add a little more for a 'cushion'
5. This becomes your par level. It should be written down – often actually on the shelves where the goods are stored. If you have a computerized system then this number can be input and orders will be made based on this stock level.

At most times of year you stick to this level of stock. Whatever is used is replaced, and no more. Hence, if you use six bottles of whisky in one week, then that's what you re-order. The following week you may only use five, so you reorder five, and so on. The only time you will need to increase your order is when usage increases or when deliveries are limited (say over Christmas and New Year). If you find that you are consistently under or overstocked then you may need to change your par level.

Branded items

The one commodity you often have to have high stocks of is branded items that have to be ordered specially. Soaps with logos, printed book matches and brochures all need ordering in large quantities because it's uneconomical to print them in small batches. So, your stocks may decline to a minimum but after a delivery you may have several months supply to store somewhere.

One thing to remember is that there can be a long 'lead time' on these (several weeks between order and delivery) so you need to place an order long enough ahead so you don't run out.

In summary:

Opposing constraints of stock control

F&B manager	**Controller**
Adequate stocks to avoid:	Minimum investment to avoid:
Refusal of menu items	Excessive capital locked up
Loss of continuity	Pilferage
Reduction of customers (and profit)	Spoilage
Loss of goodwill	Admin/space costs

Stock ratios

There are two ratios that you can use to calculate your stock levels. 'Stock days' is the number of days, on average, that it takes to use up the stock and is by far the most common in use. The other is 'stock turnover' which is how many times the stock is used (turned over) in a period.

$$\text{Stock days} \quad = \quad \frac{\text{Closing stock}}{\text{Cost per day}} \quad = \quad \text{days}$$

The cost per day is calculated by taking the usage (such as food cost of sales) and dividing it by the number of days in the period.

Here's an example: Beverage stock £3,100, cost of sales for 28 days £1,700

$$\text{Cost per day} = \quad \frac{£1,700}{28} \quad = \quad £60.71$$

$$\text{Stock days} \quad = \quad \frac{£3,100}{£60.71} \quad = \quad 51 \text{ days}$$

Fifty-one days is very long unless you have a large wine list – and a lot of money to have tied up in stock. Could it be reduced?

To work out the stock turnover:

$$\text{Stock turnover} \quad = \quad \frac{\text{Cost of sales}}{\text{Closing stock}} \quad = \quad (\text{number of times})$$

For the above example it would be:

$$\frac{£1,700}{£3,100} \quad = \quad 0.55 \text{ times per 28-day period}$$

▶▶ **ACTIVITY** ━━━━━━━━━━━━━━━━━━━━━━━━━━━━━━━━━━━━━━━

Look at stock levels in your area. Are you over-stocked, under-stocked or just about right, based on the level of usage? Are the items stored adequately according to the regulations? Are there any items of old stock that really should be disposed of?

Issuing of stock

Here again the amount of controls you have depends on the type and scale of the operation. If you have a small business and you are monitoring everything yourself then there's no need to record movements of stock – you know what's where.

In a bigger operation, however, there's much more potential for problems and also the management is more likely to want to be able to allocate accurate costs to every department – and as we saw in Chapter 4, cost control is very important to profits. Here you may need to set up a 'requisition system' which means an in-house order book. It has duplicate, numbered sheets – the top copy for ordering from the store and the second copy stays in the book (or may be passed to the Control office for checking).

The goods are then transferred from store to outlet. Financial Control will cost these out and charge the department for them. So, if £30 of paper napkins are issued to the café and £10 to the kiosk, the value of the stock changes:

> In stores reduces by £40   in the café increases by £30
> in the kiosk increases by £10

(It's a bit more double-entry book-keeping for you!)

The same can happen if goods are transferred from one unit to another

The kitchen issues £50 worth (at cost price) of sandwiches, so their stock value is reduced

The bar takes £50 worth of sandwiches to sell to customers, so their stock value is increased

Stocktaking or inventory

We normally think of inventory in terms of food and beverage because those are the most common. Food and beverage are often checked every month although many businesses are beginning to question whether this necessary if their other control systems (including par levels) are stringent enough. Daily spot-checks of key items can indicate problems just as effectively especially if computer systems are installed.

You can also count other items of inventory such as china, glass and silver, linen, cleaning materials, stationery and even maintenance items (ever tried to count light bulbs? Is this *really* a good use of your time?).

It depends on how you account for these – do you consider them 'used' when they are delivered (and so the cost is charged to the P&L) or do you keep stock of them. In any event it's often worth counting high-value items such as silver and crockery just to make sure that items aren't getting broken or lost too much.

There are two ways to count the stock – and you need to do both!

Physical count

This means actually counting every item, weighing every piece of meat and fish and assessing the quantity in every opened bottle of spirit.

If you have a bar-code reader then you can just scan most items and then download the data to computer, which will then calculate the stock and its value. Most places don't have that level of sophistication (it's expensive to install) and so you need to do a physical count and write the number of items on a list. There's an example of a spreadsheet you can use for inventory in Chapter 9 and as long as you keep the prices up to date then you will (fairly) easily be able to arrive at an accurate cost.

Theoretical count

You need to take the stock of each item – the actual physical count from the previous inventory – and add on the number delivered. You subtract any items that have been lost or damaged or wasted (including beer lost in cleaning the pipes) and then subtract the amount issued to arrive at a 'theoretical stock'. This can then be compared to the physical stock – which *should* be the same.

Here's an example for bottles of a wine:

Opening stock	11
Purchases	35
Total stock available	46
Less issued to restaurant	(32)
Less broken in cellar	(1)
Theoretical stock	13

(It's a similar calculation to cost of sales, which we did in Chapter 2 – only here you are using items rather than value)

Who should take stock?

There are different opinions as to who should actually do the inventory. Some people argue that you need an independent valuer – so an external stocktaker is hired to visit. They will count the stock, give you a valuation and also indicate which items they think are causing you problems. This service obviously costs money.

The other method is to use in-house staff who should be trained in how to count. The usual approach is to have two people do the count – one from financial control and one from the department being counted who both get to know what all the stock is and where it is kept. This method is cheaper but does mean that you have to process all the figures yourselves.

Valuation and usage calculation

The stock is normally valued at the price at which it is bought – though again there are different views on this. If you buy something that is very volatile in price then one delivery may cost you far more than another – and how do you keep track of which price you paid for which individual item? Hence some businesses always value at the latest price purchased.

We've already looked at calculating cost of sales and this closing stock valuation would form part of that. There's one more calculation to do, though, which is to find the *potential* sales from the stock you've used.

This means taking the number of items used and valuing them at their selling price. You then compare that to the actual sales you have made. This only works where you have an accurate menu-mix from EPOS or other ways of recording exactly what you sell.

Here's an example:

Number of burgers used	500
Cost price (£)	1.50
Selling price (£)	5.00
Total potential sales (£)	2,500
Total actual sales (£)	2,400
Variance (loss) (£)	100

You need to trace where this £100 of sales (which at £5 each is 20 burgers) has gone – then you realize that you transferred them to staff meals one day and forgot to do a requisition for them.

If you hadn't looked at the potential you may have not remembered – which would have meant that CoS was overstated, and staff meals undercharged.

This concludes a review of all the stock control processes that were shown in Figure 7.2. It's an enormous area – whole books have been written on it – and here you have just had an overview of different approaches. Different sectors use different methods of control, depending on their needs and also the availability of stocks – 'just in time' ordering can have a major effect on stock levels and purchasing and hence the controls needed, for instance.

Summary

In this chapter we have looked at the major aspects of controlling cash and stocks. Cash is the 'lifeblood' of the operation – businesses would fail without it – and the opportunities for loss at all stages of the control cycle are huge. Similarly with stocks – if you don't manage them effectively then high values can easily be lost. We have now looked at all the stages of cost control except usage and recipe control, which will be covered in the next chapter on standard costing. You have, therefore:

▷   Looked at all the key elements in the cycle of working capital

▷   Reviewed the ways cash can be managed both coming in and going out of the business

▷   Reviewed all the key stages of movement of stock

▷   Identified differences of attitude between operations and control.

Quiz

1.   What is liquidity?
2.   How much do you order?
3.   How do you measure stock levels?
4.   What's the best place to keep cash?
5.   What's the best way to store goods?
6.   How do you manage debtors?

8

Planning and monitoring usage

Features of raw materials ◀

Recipe costing ◀

Standard costing ◀

Standard costing for payroll ◀

Sales variances ◀

Introduction

This chapter aims to show how costs can be planned and their usage controlled through 'standard costing'. In Chapter 4 we looked at the monitoring of costs and in 5 at pricing. Here we will consider how to plan spending the correct amount on raw materials. This can be fairly complex in terms of recipes, and a loss of standards can easily cause significant cost variances.

We will then look at identifying deviations from these standards – what is due to variances in price, and what is due to variances in quantity used. We will also consider the specific problems of food and beverage materials, which can cause them to be so difficult to manage.

Standard costing techniques can also be used in other areas. We discussed the management of labour cost earlier but you can also use the technique to monitor labour cost where a flexible workforce is employed and where productivity is important to the profitability of the business. A further use for the technique is in identifying variations in revenue and considering whether differences there are due to volume or price (or both) as well.

By the end of this chapter you will, therefore, be able to:

▷   Identify the features of food and beverage raw materials that affect their controllability

▷   Discuss briefly the process for costing recipes

▷   Calculate variances according to volume and price

▷   Use the procedure for labour and other cost variances

▷   Identify differences in revenues, also due to volume and price.

Features of raw materials

We will first discuss the features of food and beverage that affect the way they are used. Although concentrating on food, many of these are also relevant for beverage.

Perishability

Food is very perishable, particularly if you use a lot of fresh produce (frozen and tinned last longer). Once cooked, health and safety requirements mean that it can be fit for consumption for only one day, and it's difficult to recycle afterwards. Menus are often designed so that food is prepared to order that can minimize this problem, but other types of facility rely on buffet-style service. Here are some examples:

▷ Carvery (popular in hotels but increasing in staff feeding facilities) which offers very quick service, low staffing costs but potential for high food cost due to lots of waste

▷ Breakfast bar in hotels – these have taken over from the fully-served breakfast. Guests help themselves to cereals, fruit, juices and bread items, so you need a good display to cater for all needs. These can deteriorate easily if not refrigerated so waste can be high here too (ever tasted 'fizzy' fruit salad that's gone off?)

▷ Lots of facilities have a salad bar, and salad items can be a major cause of food poisoning if they are not replaced frequently – and mayonnaise looks horrid when it's dried on top.

Beverage is less perishable, except for cask beer which can deteriorate rapidly if not cared for.

Desirability

The main concern is that beverage in particular is very desirable for thieves. Spirits can be easily carried out in a handbag or a large internal pocket in a jacket so physical searches of staff may often be required. A policy of staff always showing their bags and pockets whenever they leave can be helpful here. Again it's a question of attitude and management approach.

Mini-case

A trusted employee with nine years service was caught walking out with a bottle of vodka in her handbag during a routine spot-check. She lost her job and pleaded guilty when prosecuted for theft.

Processes

Food in particular has to go through a range of processes before it is ready for service – ordering, receiving, storage, issue, storage again, manufacture and then service – all of which have potential control problems. This is called the 'control cycle' and we looked at most of the stages in depth in Chapter 7. In this chapter we are just going to concentrate on the final product – the meal or the drink – and how you can ensure that these are correctly used.

Range of products

Another problem is the number of products actually on sale. Very extensive, diverse menus can be very attractive to customers (think of Chinese or Indian takeaways) but can be difficult control-wise if not carefully planned. If you don't want to cause a lot of waste then you need to ensure that there are lots of base ingredients, such as rice, which can be used in a variety of dishes. The main concern (again) is food poisoning when you have a lot of half-cooked dishes and so in order to avoid waste (and keep your customers) the menu needs careful planning.

The same is true of beverage – a large wine list looks very attractive but does it *sell*? It takes a lot of space in your cellar, costs money and eventually may deteriorate. Similarly lots of liqueurs may seem to be a good selling point but if they are rarely ordered then there's no point.

Portion and usage control

Beverage

Measures are generally used as, by law, you have to sell most items in standard quantities. The only exception is cocktails that, although they have a recipe, have fairly variable quantities. A good cocktail maker can achieve good GPs as well as having happy customers.

For standard items one way of looking at costs is to see what the 'potential' is – say from a bottle of whisky. You calculate how much you've used then see if the sales that were recorded match to this. This is also applicable for beer where you need to be careful not to pour too much into an over-sized glass, if you don't have a measured pump. And no, you can't recycle the beer where it's overflowed the glass (but you could keep it aside to see just how much is being wasted, and then pour it down the drain).

Bottles can be stamped when they leave the stores to show that they have been properly issued. This also helps prevent bar staff bringing their own bottles in for sale (and then pocketing the cash). If you are really suspicious then you can mark the bottles each day and check what's happening.

Mini-case

A popular bar had recently seen its consumption of gin rise but without any real rise in revenue. Initial suspicions were aimed at the bar staff but as several worked together it would be difficult for one to 'fiddle' without the others knowing. There was a lot of distrust, which made everybody feel very unsettled.

Eventually the manager marked the bottles with invisible pen and monitored them daily. She soon realised that it wasn't the bar staff who were the problem but the cleaner who came in early each morning when nobody else was around and filled up her hip flask. She also admitted to nibbling at the peanuts but nobody had noticed that.

Food

Portion control is crucial to good cost percentages where high volumes are involved. Take-aways often use scoops that measure out the chips, and you will always receive a standard 'squirt' of mayonnaise or ketchup (or both) on your burger. Too much and the customer may have food on their clothes (and it costs you money) – too little and they will complain of stinginess. Maintaining food cost through accurate recipe costing and usage is discussed shortly.

Mini-case

A coffee machine in a self-service airport restaurant served 2,000 cups of coffee a day. It was programmed to issue a certain volume of coffee into a cup when the button was pressed. The problem was that there was then no room for customers to add fresh milk (cream pots were OK as they have little volume) and the coffee the split on the saucer, and inevitably on the tray as well. This increased the consumption of coffee as well as of paper napkins that were used to clean up the mess.

The controller suggested reducing the measure of coffee by 10%. Result:

Room for the fresh milk

Less spillage, meaning happier customers (and so less complaints for the managers to deal with)

A saving of 10% on coffee, and a substantial amount on paper napkins. There were also savings on water and fuel for the coffee machine and the dish-washer although these couldn't be calculated.

Even for smaller operations it's important to have a standard product for both cost and customer reasons- if you bought an ice cream from a machine and saw that the person in front of you had a larger portion than you, then you'd be annoyed (and if it was your five-year-old child there'd be even more of an upset!).

You can also limit the availability of some items to stop people buying or using them. The traditional conference method is to put a token two chocolate biscuits on the communal plate – and the rest are plain (chocolate ones being more expensive). Another approach is to limit the number of sugar sachets – the more you have available the more will be used (or put in people's pockets). Fast food and in-store restaurants often don't put out sachets of ketchup and mayonnaise – the customer has to ask for them – because customers were taking them home for their own use.

▶▶ **ACTIVITY** ━━━━━━━━━━━━━━━━━━━━━━━━━━━

Be a customer somewhere such as a pub or café – and sit where you can observe the staff (at the bar is best). Watch what they do, in serving the customers and in controlling costs. Are they really efficient or just appear to be? Are they operating in the best interests of the business, or only themselves. See if you can spot wastage. Are the cash controls adequate? Go back to your facility and see if you can use anything that you've learned.

Recipe costing

Accurate costing of recipes is crucial to the entire process of food control (and beverage to a lesser extent). If you don't have standards established then there's a danger that chefs will use whatever they wish, both in terms of amount and product specification – so you may have prime steak used for a lasagne, for instance. Standard recipes are important because:

▷   A standard process is used which produces a standard quality product

▷   Training and activity rotation become easier

▷   Each customer receives a product of the same size and quality

▷   Costs remain stable

▷   Chefs know what they are doing.

This doesn't necessarily take away their creativity but just ensures they stick to basic instructions.

How the costing is done

1. The recipe is carefully worked out and a standard batch size (which could be one or 100s) is established. This means every single ingredient, including pinches of salt and half-teaspoons of spices.

2. The cost of each ingredient is calculated.

3. The costs of all ingredients for the batch are added to give a batch cost.

4. The cost per portion is calculated, and maybe the cost or GP percentage.

Recipe costs can be calculated by sophisticated computer packages that take the purchase price (from the purchasing section of the system), the yield of a commodity (such as six slices per tomato) and then convert this into a cost per dish. With computerized systems, including spreadsheets, costs can be easily amended to reflect current market prices and so update the GP.

Standard recipes are essential in many sectors. They show the catering assistant just what has to be used for a specific dish or meal and the manager knows exactly what this will cost. For sectors such as airline catering or any large-volume business this can mean a massive difference in costs.

Mini-case

A sandwich production unit presented sandwiches on plates rather than in packets – this was an upmarket operation although with very high volumes – up to 5,000 a day. The garnish on the sandwich was a lettuce leaf, a slice of cucumber and a slice of tomato. A new supervisor with little knowledge of costs decided that one slice of tomato didn't look generous enough so ordered the assistants to add one more. The cost for a single day was £158 (5,000 slices of tomato, at 6 slices per tomato = 833 tomatoes at £0.19 each). It also played havoc with the ordering processes – they had to stop adding the extra slice when they saw they were going to run out of tomatoes.

Here's an example of a recipe:

Tomato and mint sorbet

Ingredients (for 10 portions)	Recipe amount	Cost price (£)
Plum tomatoes	2 kg	1.60
Mint leaves	3 bunches	1.80
Icing sugar	425 gm	0.45
Lemon juice	1 tbsp	0.15
Total		4.00
Cost per portion		0.40
Selling price at 65% gross profit		1.14

Standard costing

Standard costing is a term normally used for finding out the budget – 'standard' – cost of a recipe according to the exact recipe specification. Once you have standard recipe costs established then you can compare them to what actually occurs and see where differences appear. You can show whether any change in cost for producing an item is due to differences in use of ingredients or in the price of them.

For some sectors this may not be important but in sectors with very tight margins and high volumes, such as inflite catering, any slight variances may mean the difference between profit and loss on a contract. Once you know about the technique you can use it to manipulate your estimates – and perhaps see the financial effect of different specifications. It can also be used for analysing variances in labour and sales and we'll look at these later in the chapter.

Understanding, and calculating, the technique can seem quite complicated so we will work through this step by step.

How to do it

Let's look at the production of a menu item – say scrambled eggs. For 10 portions of scrambled eggs you need 20 eggs (we'll ignore the butter for cooking) which cost £0.10 each.

If you showed the cost of these in a diagram it would look like Figure 8.1.

Figure 8.1 Basic cost

But if we were to use five extra eggs as ingredients for the same number of portions (we were generous) then this would cost more, see Figure 8.2.

This extra cost would mean that the scrambled eggs would cost £2.50 instead of £2.00 for the same 10 portions without any extra sales.

Figure 8.2 Basic cost plus extra usage

The other problem could be that an egg shortage caused a price rise or that the chef decided to use organic rather than free range. The extra 2 pence per egg (now 12p instead of 10p) obviously affects all those 25 eggs that you are now using, see Figure 8.3.

Figure 8.3 Basic cost plus extra usage and extra price

This means that although you originally costed or budgeted for £2.00 (the 'standard cost') the actual cost was £3.00.

Methods of standard costing

There are two methods of calculating standard cost variances, both of which produce the same result. Different people use different methods, so choose the one that suits you best.

Here's the first way of doing it. Books tend to be a bit theoretical when showing this which can be off-putting but if you go through step-by-step then it's not too tedious.

Method 1

This finds the difference first and then calculates its cost.

1. Find the budgeted (standard) usage of each ingredient from the standard recipe

2.   Calculate the cost of each ingredient

3.   Calculate the cost of the ingredients that were actually used

Now you can find the variances.

4.   Find the usage variance by taking the *difference* in ingredients times the *standard* (budgeted, or original) price

5.   Find the price variance by taking the difference in price of the ingredients times the Actual quantity (the amount used)

It's easier if you see an example (using those scrambled eggs again):

	Ingredients	Price (£)	Cost (£)		
Budget (recipe says)	20 eggs	@ 0.10	2.00		should have cost
Actual	25 eggs	@ 0.12	3.00		actually did cost
Variance		0.02	1.00	ADVERSE	spent too much

The difference is expressed as favourable (good) or adverse (bad) or FAV and ADV for short

These are Steps 1 to 3 as above. So you know the total variance is £1.00 (adverse), but how much of this is due to volume (quantity of eggs here) and how much to extra price?

			(£)	
Step 4 – Usage Variance	5 eggs	@ 0.10	0.50	ADV
Step 5 – Price Variance	25 eggs	@ 0.02	0.50	ADV
		total	1.00	ADV

Look at the three diagrams (Figures 8.1-3) if it helps – Steps 1 and 2 are the Budget, Step 4 adds the extra usage, Step 5 adds the extra price, which all adds up to the Actual result (Step 3).

Method 2

This calculates the value first and then finds the variance:

1.   Take the standard quantity (recipe ingredients) and multiply it by the standard (budget) price

In textbooks this is Standard Quantity × Standard Price or STDQ × STDP

2.   Change the quantity to what you actually used:

Actual quantity × standard price (ACTQ × STDP)

3.   Find the difference between the two – this is the usage variance

4.   Change the price to what you actually paid:

Actual quantity × actual price (ACT Q × ACT P)

5.   Find the difference between the two – this is the price variance.

So, using the above example:

STDQ × STDP	=	20 eggs × £0.10	=	£2.00	
ACTQ × STDP	=	25 eggs × £0.10	=	£2.50	
Usage variance			=	£0.50	ADV
ACTQ × ACTP	=	25 eggs × £0.12	=	£3.00	
Price variance			=	£0.50	ADV
Total variance			=	£1.00	ADV

Let's try another example – simplified to just one ingredient although in practice most recipes have several ingredients all of which can vary in usage and price.

	Cost (£)	Usage	Total (£)	
Budget food cost	4.80	140	672.00	
Actual food cost	4.70	130	611.00	
Difference	0.10	10	61.00	FAV
Budget quantity x budget price	140 × £4.80 =		672.00	
Actual quantity x budget price	130 × £4.80 =		624.00	
			48.00	FAV
Actual quantity x actual price	130 × £4.70 =		611.00	
			13.00	FAV
			61.00	FAV

Exercise

Here's the budget food cost of two ingredients, so now it's your turn!

Ingredient F – 0.25 kg per portion at £2.00 per kg, a total of 255 kg is used, total cost £510

Ingredient O – 0.125 kg per portion at £2.40 per kg, a total of 127.5 kg is used, total cost £306

So the total budgeted cost is £816.00. The actual food cost for the ingredients is:

Actual food cost	kg	£/kg	Per portion (£)	usage (kg)	total (£)
F	0.26	£.90	0.49	265.2	503.88
O	0.175	2.60	0.46	178.5	464.10
	Total		0.95		967.98

Where has the extra £151.98 cost (the difference between £816.00 and £967.98) occurred?

TIP

The recipe has two ingredients, so you will need to work them out separately. You can then add the total variances together to find out the overall difference.

Answer

Item F			(£)	
Budget quantity x budget price	255 x £2.00	=	510.00	
Actual quantity x budget price	265.2 x £2.00	=	<u>530.40</u>	
			20.40	ADV
Actual quantity x actual price	265.2 x £1.90	=	<u>503.88</u>	
			<u>26.52</u>	FAV
Total F			6.12	FAV
Item O				
Budget quantity x budget price	127.5 x £2.40	=	306.00	
Actual quantity x budget price	178.5 x £2.40	=	<u>428.40</u>	
			122.40	ADV
Actual quantity x actual price	178.5 x £2.60	=	<u>£464.10</u>	
			<u>£35.70</u>	ADV
Total O			<u>£158.10</u>	ADV
TOTAL RECIPE			£151.98	ADV

Can you identify where the major problem has occurred?

It's the ingredient O and is in the actual quantity used – but the price is a problem too. The quantity of ingredient F increased a little but compensated by costing slightly less per kilogram.

▶▶ **ACTIVITY**

Look at a food item that you are involved in (or can see in a restaurant). Can you calculate how much extra cost there would be if you used too much?

The technique works for price falls as well as rises. What about using too little, or if prices are lower – is this a problem? Well, accounting wise it may not be (you've cut costs) but this is a quality issue. You need to maintain your quality standards so your customers know what to expect. Cutting costs can harm the business long-term – what you want is to be more efficient in what you use, rather than wasting resources.

Standard costing for payroll

We've concentrated on F&B, which is the most common area where standard costing is used but we can also use the technique for other areas.

As we've seen, payroll is traditionally fairly fixed but businesses are now trying to be more flexible in their scheduling, hopefully without upsetting staff.

First let's use the standard costing way of finding differences in the cost of overall payroll.

Here's a budget and actual staff cost for two jobs:

Budget staff cost	Hourly rate (£)	Hours	Total (£)
Catering assistants	5.00	120	600.00
General assistants	4.50	160	720.00
Total			1,320.00
Actual staff cost			
Catering assistants	5.10	110	561.00
General assistants	4.40	170	748.00
Total			1,309.00
OVERALL COST DIFFERENCE			£11.00 FAV

Can you work out for each categoru how much of the difference is related to pay rate and how much to the number of hours worked?

Answer

Catering assistants			(£)	
Budget hours x budget rate	120 x £5.00	=	600.00	
Actual hours x budget rate	110 x £5.00	=	550.00	
Difference due to hours			50.00	FAV
Actual hours x actual rate	110 x £5.10	=	561.00	
Difference due to hours			11.00	ADV
Total			39.00	FAV
General assistants				
Budget hours x budget rate	160 x £4.50	=	720.00	
Actual hours x budget rate	170 x £4.50	=	765.00	
Difference due to hours			45.00	ADV
Actual hours x actual rate	170 x £4.40	=	748.00	
Difference due to hours			17.00	FAV
Total			28.00	ADV
TOTAL			11.00	FAV

You could also use it to plan ahead. If you have a current situation of staff working certain hours at a set rate and a proposal is made to change these, then the same type of exercise can be performed.

Here's a scenario you could use. The housekeeping manager employs cleaners for 300 student rooms. Each cleaner is expected to clean 25 rooms a day at a cost of £1.20 per room per day (including benefits).

However, a new agreement is proposed by the staff union which suggests a pay increase of 5% and a reduction of the number of rooms cleaned to 24 per day. How much would each of these options cost? What would be the difference for each change (reduction of rooms and pay increase)?

Sales variances

All the above have been costs – but what about using the technique for sales too? Let's try this with a package price for a holiday. We can see what the effect would be on sales if we decided to offer a £50 discount per holiday.

	Normal Budget	Forecast with discount	Variance
Holiday guests	1,350	1,550	200
Package price	£500	£450	(£50)
Sales	£675,000	£697,500	£22,500

Now lets calculate how much of these extra £22,500 sales are due to extra people, and how much was lost due to the discount).

	Rooms	Rate	Revenue
Guests – budget			
Guests- forecast			
Variance			
Volume (usage)			
Price			
Total			

Remember that it's easier to find the usage variance first, then the price.

Here's another exercise to try – this time for a meal.

	Covers	Selling price	Revenue
Budget	3,320	£3.75	
Actual	3,170	£3.80	
Variance			
Volume (usage)			
Price			
Total			

Answer

	Covers	Selling price (£)	Revenue (£)	
Budget	3,320	3.75	12,450.00	
Actual	3,170	3.80	12,046.00	
Variance	(150)	0.05	404.00	ADV
Volume (usage)	(150)	3.75	562.50	ADV
Price	3,170	0.05	158.50	FAV
Total			404.00	ADV

Now try and exercise on accommodation

	Rooms	Selling price	Revenue
Budget	50	£49.50	
Actual	55	£47.50	
Variance			
Volume (usage)			
Price			
Total			

Answer

	Rooms	Selling price (£)	Revenue (£)	
Budget	50	49.50	2,475.00	
Actual	55	47.50	2,612.50	
Variance	5	(2.00)	137.50	FAV
Volume (usage)	5	49.50	247.50	FAV
Price	55	(2.00)	110.00	ADV
Total			137.50	FAV

There's also a technique described in the textbooks called Flexible Budgets. By combining the two techniques, you can compare the GP levels as well.

▶▶ ACTIVITY

Talk to managers in your organization. Do they use standard costing as a technique or isn't it of relevance? If they don't, could they?

Why not try looking at payroll costs or at sales and see if you can analyse variances using this approach?

Summary

In this eighth chapter we have discussed the technique of standard costing which is mainly used for analysing variances for recipes. The differences relating to usage and to price of the ingredients can be separately identified so that the manager can then take action where possible.

Standard costing can also be used for other purposes. It can show where payroll costs have not matched budget, again identifying variances due to volume (number of staff, or hours worked) and price (rates of pay). Additionally it can be used to analyse variances in sales revenue, also showing where shortfalls or overages have occurred in average spends and in customer numbers. These can be used in all sectors of the industry – for leisure and tourism as well as food and beverage and rooms areas.

You have, therefore:

▷ Discussed the purpose of standard recipes

▷ Reviewed in diagrammatic format the way that standard costs are identified

▷ Calculated variances due to volume and price

▷ Identified other areas where the technique might be used

▷ Calculated a range of other variances.

Quiz

1. What do 'standard quantity' and 'standard price' mean?

2. Why is a standard recipe important for airline catering?

3. How can standard costing be used in a rooms department's sales variance analysis?

4. How can standard costing help to predict payroll costs?

5. What are the two approaches to standard costing?

9

Using spreadsheets for management tasks

Introduction

In this chapter we are going to see how using spreadsheets can help you with many of the control tasks that we have discussed in the different chapters. We'll also see how you can use graphs and charts (hand-drawn and by spreadsheet) to help in decision-making and presenting results.

We will look at some of the simple techniques that can make spreadsheets easier to use on a frequent basis and at some of the shortcuts you can take. Incorporating some basic design features can help with ongoing usage, and with enabling others to use spreadsheets that you have designed. The use of charts and how they can help with presenting complex information in a simpler way will also be considered.

It's assumed that you have a basic knowledge of spreadsheets. If some of this is boring because you're at a higher level of competence, then please move on. There's a refresher exercise to revise skills and perhaps practise some new ones and some suggestions about using spreadsheets for personal tasks.

By the end of this chapter, therefore, you should be able to:

▷   Comprehend the basic principles of spreadsheet design

▷   Practise a range of techniques to improve speed and efficiency

▷   Comprehend the variety of areas where spreadsheets can be used

▷   Draw a graph to scale by hand

▷   Create a graph using a spreadsheet.

The basics of spreadsheet design

The following basic principles are adapted from Peter Harris' book '*Profit Planning*' – see the reading list for further details. They are:

▷   Design on paper first

▷   Use separate Input and Output worksheets

▷   And maybe another for 'workings out' (or at the end of the Input area)

▷   Test your results.

Designing on paper

The temptation with doing a spreadsheet is just to sit at the computer and do it, without planning. This works for some people, but can waste a lot of time.

If you take a piece of scrap paper (recycled, of course!) and write down all the things you need to do for this particular spreadsheet, you'll have a better idea of how much space it's going to take.

Ask yourself the following questions:

▷ What's the purpose of this spreadsheet? Is it very complex?

▷ Who is going to use it – just you or lots of other people? If it's others will they need instructions about how to use it?

▷ Do you trust their skills?

▷ Will the spreadsheet need to be significantly amended at a future date, or just updated?

▷ How many reports need to be generated from one batch of input data?

▷ Do you need several different worksheets within the same file?

▷ Are you going to have to link this spreadsheet file to another?

▷ Is there a requirement for the report/s to fit in a specific space, such as an A4 piece of paper?

▷ Do you need colour and different fonts?

▷ What about charts?

▷ Are you going to have to copy a chart into another file (e.g. Word)?

▷ If you're really skilled, what about macros? Hyperlinks?

And so on…..

Once you've done this then you can make a design – still on paper, though. You can roughly sketch out what will go where on the different worksheets. Some textbooks suggest actually working out the formulas although with all the techniques available now (Copy, Drag, Move and so on) there isn't normally a need to do this.

Try and make it as easy to use as possible with columnar formats (working in parallel with the same columns as you move down) and using the top left-hand corner of the screen first, then paging down rather than across.

▼
▼
TIP

If you can, work out the results by hand first – then you can check these against output from the spreadsheet.

Input and Output areas

Using separate Input and Output worksheets, and maybe another for 'workings out', means that:

▷   You keep all your raw data (INPUT – your original numbers – those that you key in) separate from

▷   All the OUTPUT which is the results. Output areas are all formulae – no actual figures are keyed in there.

Ideally you have a separate worksheet within the file for the input, and then several for output depending on what type of reports you need. For instance, for a P&L, the input would be the trial balance (all the source data you need) and the output the departmental reports, possibly each on a separate worksheet. The front page would then be a total of all the departmental reports. This means that the source data (TB) only gets entered once and, when updated each month, immediately change all the reports – much easier than moving around lots of different worksheets.

Here's an example for a very small P&L statement:

INPUT

This is your source data – it's raw numbers – on one worksheet (could be actually called 'Input' if you wish, or perhaps 'source data'):

Input worksheet:

Cell	A	B
1	Sales including VAT	28200
2	Payroll	6800
3	Expenses	2400
4	Customers	5000
5	Capacity	6000
6	VAT rate	0.175

Workings out

Any intermediate calculations you need to do (for instance, extract VAT). This could be a separate worksheet or just further down the input column.

Here you type in the formula to extract the VAT from the sales.

Cell	A	B	Formula in B	
1	Sales less VAT	24,000	= B1-(B1*B6)	(formatted as £)

Now you have the net figures that you need, ready to do the P&L.

OUTPUT

These are *results* and are calculated by formula *from the input screen* – there is *no* source data in the output worksheet.

Cell	A	B	Formula in B	
1	Sales	£24,000	= Input!B10	(formatted as £)
2	Payroll	(£6,800)	= -Input!B2	(formatted as £)
3	Expenses	(£2,400)	= -Input!B3	(formatted as £)
4	Profit	£14,800	= sum(B1:B3)	(formatted as £)
5	Average spend per customer	£4.80	= B1/Input!B4	(formatted as £)
6	Occupancy	83.3%	= Input!B4/Input!B5	(formatted as %)
7	Profit per customer	£2.96	= B4/ Input!B4	(formatted as £)
8	Profit percentage	61.7%	= B4/B1	(formatted as %)

(Where it says 'Input' in the B cells above it means that the spreadsheet has gone to the input worksheet to get the data from the particular cell. So – B1 in the output worksheet has looked in cell B10 in the input worksheet to find the number 24000.)

►► ACTIVITY

Choose one of the earlier exercises and plan on paper how it would look on a spreadsheet.

Spreadsheet exercise

Objective: to practise many of the basic spreadsheet skills using Excel in order to create a Rooms departmental statement and utilize the basic spreadsheet design principles. You will also create a simple pie chart.

This is what you want to achieve (rows 1-5 are *input*, 7-13 onwards are *output*):

Cell	A	B	C
1	Rooms revenue	12000	
2	Payroll	1680	
3	Expenses	940	
4	Rooms sold	150	
5	Rooms available	200	
6			
7	**Rooms P&L**		
8	Rooms revenue	£12,000	100.0%
9	Payroll	£(1,680)	14.0%
10	Expenses	£(940)	7.8%
11	Rooms profit	£9,380	78.2%
12	Average room rate	£80.00	
13	Room occupancy	75.0%	

You will see that some items appear twice. This is because of the design features we discussed earlier where we are trying to keep the raw data (input) separate from the results (output), which makes it easier to manage the spreadsheet. This is particularly relevant when you have very large reports.

Note: Click – means use the left button of the mouse, means Enter

1   *Start a new worksheet.* Start Excel. Click the new file icon or use the File, New command.

2   *Type the labels as above.* Starting at cell A1, type rooms revenue, and press [Enter]. Note that the cursor automatically moves to cell A2. Continue to type all the labels

3   *Adjust the column widths.* Put the cursor on the line between the titles of columns A and B (grey shaded) until you see a black cross. Hold the mouse down and move it to the right until the column widens enough for your needs

4   *Embolden the word Profit.* Cell A11; the word 'Profit'. Click the Bold icon or use the Format, Cell, Font, Bold command

5   *Italicize the source data cells.* Block A1 to B5 as above, click on Italic icon

6   *Underline rooms department statement.* Cell A7, block the words and Underline

7   *Enter the raw data.* Type in the numbers as shown in B1-B5 *only*. Save the file

8   *Create the departmental statement – start with the rooms revenue.* Go to B8, type the formula =B1 and press [Enter]. You will see that the cell says '12000'.

9   *Repeat for the payroll.* Go to B9, type the formula = B2 and press [Enter]. BUT
     – as this is a cost you really want to subtract this from the revenue, so you
     need to Edit the formula. You will see the formula displayed in a long space
     below the tool bar. Click on this and move the cursor between the = and the
     B. Insert a minus sign and press [Enter]. You will see that cell B9 now says (1680)
     or -1680, depending on the set-up of your machine.

10   *Enter expense formula.* You can do this in two ways. Click on the B9 cell and
     either Copy (icon or Edit, Copy) and then Paste to B10, or Fill Down to the
     next cell. You need to make sure if you are Filling Down that a little black
     cross appears on the bottom right-hand corner of B9 – this indicates the
     correct function is being used. Note that the formula in B10 is correct and
     the number (-940) displayed

11   *Calculate the profit.* Cell B11. Click on the Sum icon – it will suggest the range
     of cells to add together. If this is fine then press [Enter], if not then select
     the correct range and then press [Enter]. This will add the revenue, and
     subtract the costs, to give a profit.

12   *Format these as Currency.* Select B8 to B11. Click on the Currency icon. You
     really need these as round pounds (no pence) so click twice on the Decrease
     decimal icon on the toolbar. If the costs are now set up as a minus and you
     wanted brackets you can change this using Format, Cell, Number, Currency,
     then choose an option that displays both £ and ( ), if you have it available.

13   *Calculate the Average Room rate.* Cell B12. The formula is =B8/B4 (Rooms
     revenue divided by rooms sold). Format this as Currency to 2 decimal places

14   *Calculate the Room Occupancy.* Cell B13. You don't have to type the cell
     references. If you type = and then click on cell B4, type / then click on cell
     B5 press [Enter] you will enter the formula more quickly. Format as a
     Percentage to 1 decimal place (note that if you format as % you don't need
     to use the x100 or /100 as you would if you calculated by hand)

15   *Align the figures to the right of their cells if necessary.* Select B8:B12 and click on
     the Align Right icon

16   *Calculate the costs and profits as a percentage of sales.* Cell C9. Enter formula =B9/
     B8, format as % to one decimal as a percentage of sales point. Copy to the
     next cell down. Look at the result in C10 – it isn't correct and you'll see that
     it says =B10/B9. You need to FIX the cell reference of B8 so that all items

calculate as a percentage of this. Go back to C9 and Edit the formula to read = B9/B$8. Then fill this down to C10 and C11.

You will now see that each cell refers to B8 – the $ sign fixes the cell reference. Here we used it to fix the Row, but you can also fix the Column by putting a $ in front of the column letter, or fix both.

If you wish you can copy the formula back to C8, the rooms revenue expressed as a % of itself

17   *Check the alignment of the percentages (should be Right).* If necessary, correct these

18   *Change the font for the entire worksheet.* Click on the grey square above the row titles and to the left of the column titles – this will block everything. Click on the font title above and format both font and size to a style you prefer.

19   *Save your file again.* Congratulations – you have now created a simple profit statement!

Now, suppose you wanted to put this information into a chart format. The best way to display this information would be a Pie Chart. I know we haven't talked about these yet but it's a chance to practise using the Chart Wizard.

1   *Select the data.* Highlight A9 to B11

2   *Use Chart Wizard.* Click on the Chart Wizard icon (looks like a bar chart)

3   *Choose your chart type.* Click on Pie, then Next to see the chart, then Next again

4   *Title your chart.* In the Chart Title box type 'Rooms P&L', click Next

5   *Save it.* Save as a new chart in Chart1 (note that if you wanted to copy and paste the chart later into a Word document you would be best to use the Save As Object option). Click on Finish

6   *Change the font.* For the whole chart, click anywhere (you should see black dots appear around the whole chart. Select a font and size as desired.

7   *Move the legend box.* Click on the legend box (black dots should surround just this item) and then drag it to where you wish to position it. If you wanted to change the font of just the box, then you would click on the box, not the entire chart

8   *Save your file*

Using spreadsheets for different tasks

Now we need to look at using spreadsheets for different jobs. Here are some exercises that you can try yourself if you have access to a spreadsheet.

Calculating ratios

We have already done some above. Why not take the Food and Beverage exercise from Chapter 4and see if you can set it up on a spreadsheet? The information from the question goes into the Input area, and then the Output is the report and the ratios. You may not need a 'workings out' section here.

Pricing

You can use spreadsheets for pricing in different ways – depending on what type of pricing method you use. Later on, when we look at charts, we will practise setting up a break-even chart. Here are a couple of examples of how you can calculate prices using the GP method and the Contribution method.

First, GP – suppose you had costs of £4.00 and wanted to see the price that would emerge at different levels of GP%.

Source data

Cell	A	B	C	D
1	Costs	£4.00		
2		Scenario 1	Scenario 2	Scenario 3
3	Gross Profit required	30%	40%	50%
4	Cost percentage	70%	60%	50%
5				
6	Vat rate	17.50%		

Now here's the Output area which calculates the selling price, and the menu price including VAT.

Cell	A	B	C	D
11	Cost level	=B4	=C4	=D4
12	Selling price	=$B1/B11	=$B1/C11	=$B1/D11
13	Menu price with VAT	=B12*(1+$B6)	=C12*(1+$B6)	=D12*(1+$B6)

Note that the 'grossing up' technique is used (taking the cost and dividing it by the cost % to achieve the SP). So the answer will show as:

Cell	A	B	C	D
11	Cost level	70%	60%	50%
12	Selling price	£5.71	£6.67	£8.00
13	Menu price with VAT	£6.71	£7.84	£9.40

A couple of extra tips for you.

Use of the $ sign

This 'fixes' the cell reference. You notice that every SP calculation needs the basic cost figure (£4.00) which is in cell B2. If you set up the correct formula in cell B12 AND include the $ sign as shown then you can copy (or Fill Right) the cell across. The B column stays fixed but the second half of the formula changes to the C and D columns.

The action is repeated to add the VAT.

▷   Putting the $ in front of the column – fixes the column reference

▷   Putting the $ in front of the row – fixes the row reference

▷   Putting the $ in front of both – fixes both

This saves a lot of time when building complex sheets. You just need to double-check the formula in the new cells.

Calculating VAT (or adding any percentage figure on to a base)

You'll see that the formula reads * (times) and then in brackets (1+) and the cell reference (such as 1+C14). This says take the original amount and multiply it by itself and the percentage amount of the cell (here 17.5%). It's the same as using a calculator where you multiply by 1.175 to add VAT. If you wanted to add 20% to the total then the formula would be * (1+ 20%).

Next – an example for the contribution method. Suppose you have variable costs of £25 and want to see what contribution percentage can be achieved at different sales levels – say £70, £75 and £80 (we'll ignore VAT this time, but you could extract it by dividing by 1+ 17.5%).

Here's the source data:

Cell	A	B	C	D
3	Variable costs	£25		
4				
5	Selling price	£70	£75	£80

The answer is:

Cell	A	B	C	D
11	Selling price	£70	£75	£80
12	Variable costs	-£25	-£25	-£25
13	Contribution	£45	£50	£55
14				
15	CM percentage	64.3%	66.7%	68.8%

The formulas are:

Cell	A	B	C	D
11	Selling price	=B5	=C5	=D5
12	Variable costs	=-$B3	=-$B3	=-$B3
13	Contribution	=SUM(B11:B12)	=SUM(C11:C12)	=SUM(D11:D12)
14				
15	CM percentage	=B13/B11	=C13/C11	=D13/D11

You'll see that the variable cost formula has a minus sign in front of the $B which then means that it is subtracted (and shows in red if you have a colour screen and printer). The percentage takes the CM as a % of sales and is formatted as a percentage to 1 decimal place (the % icon).

These are rather simple as examples and for one calculation a calculator may be quicker – but if you have lots to do then it's worth setting up. Once you have the formulas established for one item then you can copy for other items – providing that the $ signs are set correctly.

Stocktaking

Lots of you may already have stock control packages, perhaps even bar-code scanners to scan items which then automatically download to computer. This will update the stock list, calculate inventories and then give a total stock value. Other, smaller businesses don't! You can use a spreadsheet to calculate your stock values, but you do need to take care.

This may be one situation in which you don't use an input area, given the number of additions you may need to make each time for new items. If your inventory is stable (that is, you don't add new items, or new sizes) then you may be able to use one area for input and another for output.

Columns	Commodity	Unit size	Price	Quantity	Value

It's suggested that you write-protect those columns you don't need to use often, depending on how reliable your inputting is (or somebody else's).

You could use a separate worksheet for each area (kitchen, stores, restaurants, etc.) and then another to total them all. You may also want to separate the commodities (meat, fish, dairy, tinned goods, and so on) in which case your summary sheet might look like Table 9.1.

	Stores	Kitchen	Restaurant	Bar food	TOTAL COMMODITY
Meat and fish					
Dairy					
Bakery					
Tinned goods					
Frozen foods					
Herbs and spices					
Prepared foods					
Snacks					
Miscellaneous					
Drink for cooking					
TOTAL STOCK					

Table 9.1   Sample summary sheet

Each cell should contain a formula that takes the relevant total from the relevant stock sheet, so that if you amend your sheets or stock then the figures will stay accurate. The total columns then SUM the rows or columns.

To calculate the overall Cost of Sales you need the standard formula, given in Chapter 2 when we discussed the PandL report (see page 38).

If you have an EPOS system then the sales report may also give you a theoretical cost of sales figure, based on your menus and pricing system.

You can also use a spreadsheet to calculate the items *used* and then their value. This is really useful for high-value items such as wine. For instance:

Commodity	Opening Stock	Plus purchases	Less transfers	Less closing stock	Cost	Value of stock used
Whisky						
Gin						

The value of the stock used can then be compared to the sales achieved, by different commodity, so you can see whether there are losses.

Forecasting

Spreadsheets can be really helpful for saving time in projecting sales and profits, say for a week, based on changing volumes and sales.

For instance (fill in some source data yourself):

	Mon.	Tues.	Wed.	Thurs.	Fri.	Sat.	Sun.
Visitors							
Spend							
Variable cost							
Fixed cost							

Note that fixed costs *per day* and the variable costs *per visitor* remain unchanged, so that you can treat all this as input data. Only the number of visitors would change, so the output would look like this:

	Mon.	Tues.	Wed.	Thurs.	Fri.	Sat.	Sun.	Total
Visitors								
Sales								
Variable costs								
Contribution								
Fixed costs								
Profit								
Break-even point								

You can then see that some days make more profit, others less, and can plan accordingly.

▶▶ ACTIVITY

If you have access to a spreadsheet then try setting this one up, practising all we've talked about so far. If you haven't got access, then you could just use a calculator.

Market segmentation

If you're in a rooms department in a hotel you may have lots of market segments all of which vary by day and by week. For this you can set up really complex formulas to analyse revenue and occupancy by day, and then show the patterns over a period.

For instance, another activity:

Rooms sold (fill some numbers in yourself if you wish)

	Mon.	Tues.	Wed.	Thurs.	Fri.	Sat.	Sun.
Rooms available	100	100	100	100	100	100	100
Rack rate							
Tour							
Corporate							

Room occupancy (calculate the percentages)

	Mon.	Tues.	Wed.	Thurs.	Fri.	Sat.	Sun.
Rooms available	100	100	100	100	100	100	100
Rack rate							
Tour							
Corporate							

By manipulating the percentages you can see how much revenue you can generate so please add some average room rates and then calculate the revenues.

Room rate and revenue

	Mon.	Tues.	Wed.	Thurs.	Fri.	Sat.	Sun.
Avg. room rate							
Rack rate							
Tour							
Corporate							
Revenue							
Rack rate							
Tour							
Corporate							

Presenting results

Now let's look at charts and how you can use them for forecasting and reporting figures. Some charts are best drawn by hand but a computer (usually spreadsheet) is good for display, especially if you can add colour. In this section we'll show you how you can use graphs and charts to help you display information for decision-making and for presentation.

There are three main types that are likely to be of benefit to you – pie charts, bar charts and line charts.

Pie charts

These are useful for splitting something into component parts – like slices of a pie. So, we can use it for splitting total customers into market segments or total sales into different types. We can also split the 'sales pie' into different costs and profit. We practised one earlier as part of the spreadsheet exercise. Figure 9.1 shows an example.

Figure 9.1 Pie chart

Bar charts

Bar charts can show comparative numbers, day-by-day or week-by-week, for example. You can show two sets of numbers side by side as well. Depending on the type of data you can show them either vertically or horizontally. They are good for showing changes in staffing levels or for forecasting. Figure 9.2 is an example (this is actually a column chart but is always known as a bar chart):

Figure 9.2 Bar chart

Line charts

This can be either a single zig-zag line to show, for instance, sales levels or several lines to show different items. A break-even chart is a line chart, which we'll look at shortly. Figure 9.3 shows a line chart used for sales figures.

Figure 9.3 Line chart

Charts for decision making

Here you want to be accurate – a chart is a *tool* here rather than just a picture. It's worth taking time over so that it really will 'add value' to your decisions. For instance, if you were trying to find out the BEP you would want it to show exactly where the sales exceed the total costs – the exact BEP. Having approximate figures just isn't good enough, which is what a spreadsheet version will give you. It's also useful to be able to look at different scenarios – for instance to plot different sales lines for different selling prices, all with the same costs. This will then give you three alternative BEPs.

Figure 9.4 shows what a break-even chart looks like.

Figure 9.4 Break-even chart

Note: Units could be customers or numbers of items, like cups of coffee.

The Y-axis (vertical – the letter stands up!) is the sales and costs in money. The X-axis (horizontal) is the volume in units.

The main diagonal line from the zero point is sales because for every one you sell you have an extra amount of sales.

The horizontal line parallel to the X-axis is the fixed costs – you have the cost if your volume of sales is zero, but the same cost if you have a high volume. The variable costs then get added on TOP of this fixed cost line because you need to find the total costs if you want the BEP. As the variable costs start at 0 (no sales = no variable costs) the starting point is the FC line. It then goes diagonally upwards.

The point where the total cost line is crossed by the sales line is the BEP – here sales exceed costs, so you are then into profit.

It will make more sense if you draw one yourself. If you draw this really accurately on graph paper you can read off the scale the exact BEP. You can also read off how much profit you can make at different levels of volume.

▶▶ **ACTIVITY**

Get some graph paper if possible. Otherwise ordinary lined paper will do but just needs a bit more care in measuring and ruling. You'll also need a sharp pencil and a ruler.

Draw a graph using the following data:

Selling price £12.00	
Contribution 25%	
Fixed costs	£7,200
Customers	4,000

(It will help if you work out the totals first before you plan your graph)

How to do it by hand

1 *Work out the sales.* Customers x Selling price (= £48,000)

2 *Work out the contribution.* Sales x CM% (= £12,000)

3 *Work out the variable costs.* Sales less contribution (= £36,000)

4 *Work out the total costs.* Variable + fixed costs (= £43,200)

5 *Draw the axes for the chart.* On a piece of paper, placed in landscape position,

6   *Decide on the scale.* This needs to be enough to accommodate sales of £48,000 on the Y axis and volume of 4,000 on the X axis. Mark off the intermediate points on the scale (say every £5,000 on the Y and every 500 on X). The corner of the L where the X meets the Y is the zero (0) point. Label the axes.

7   *Draw the Sales Line.* Find the point on the top right corner where £48,000 on the Y meets 4,000 on the X. From that point draw a line with a ruler back to 0 (it should look roughly diagonal). Label this line.

8   *Draw the fixed cost line.* Find the point on the Y-axis at 0 volume where the costs would equal £7,000. Draw a line horizontal to the X-axis at this level (in other words, the end point on the far right is also at £7,200). Label this line.

9   *Draw the total cost line.* This touches the Y-axis at the point where the fixed cost line starts – that is, at £7,200 at 0 volume. It ends on the right side at £43,200 and 4,000 volume. If in doubt look at the BE chart diagram in the workbook. Label this line.

10   *The point where this line crosses.* Label this point *the sales line is the break-even point.*

11   *Title the chart.* Give it a short name that is meaningful, then save the file.

You may want to offer a discount and need to see the effect on the BEP – in other words, how many more you would need to sell at a reduced price. You can add a new line to your graph for this, and again read off the BEP.

You could also see the effect of putting prices up without raising costs.

How to do a break-even chart on a spreadsheet

This assumes you have already done the exercises above and know a little about the Chart Wizard.

This is the data you will need set up on the spreadsheet

	A	B	C
1	Data for graph		
2		start	finish
3	Sales	0	£48,000
4	Fixed costs	£7,200	£7,200
5	Total costs	£7,200	£43,200

1   *Set up the required data.* On Excel, input the data as above (or use the source data from the question and calculate these out).

2   *Select the data.* Highlight the titles and amounts for Sales, Fixed and Total costs (A3:C5).

3   *Use Chart Wizard.* Click on the ChartWizard icon. Select a Line chart and choose the first type and click Next.

4   *Correct the display.* Click on (Series in..) Rows, then Next.

5   *Add the titles.* Chart title is 'Break-even chart'; X-axis is 'Volume'; Y-axis is 'Sales and Costs'. Then click Next.

6   *Place the chart where you need it.* Then click Finish.

7   *Format the fonts for the chart and the title.* Click on the whole chart then Format, Selected Chart Area, and the font you wish for the whole chart. Click on the title itself then format that for a larger size font and in bold.

8   *Look and see if the lines start at 0 on the Y axis. If not then you need to amend this.* Click on the X-axis and Format, Selected Axis, Scale. The value Axis should NOT 'cross between categories' – so if ticked then un-tick it.

9   *Notice that the scale on X is only 1 and 2.* Go back to the source data on the spreadsheet. Insert 4 new columns between B and C. On the Sales and Total cost lines type intervening numbers 10,000, 20,000, 30,000, 40,000 and on the Fixed cost line 7,200 in each cell. This should include them in the scale.

10 *Do any more tidying that you wish, and save the file.*

Other types of charts

A charts done by a spreadsheet is a picture – it gives you an instant appreciation of what you are trying to say, far more easily than words. Charts can be very useful for presenting results in a meeting, where it's the overall impression you're trying to give, not an exact result. Here are some more ideas.

Bar (or column) charts

Most other charts are used to show trends – say in bookings. You've seen how to do a bar chart already but you could also compare actual customers to booked – so you see what proportion are chance guests. If you can do this over a week you could see if there's any difference from day to day.

This is how it would look in a table – boring!

Day	Booked	Chance	Total
Monday	2	8	10
Tuesday	2	10	12
Wednesday	6	14	20
Thursday	10	14	24
Friday	30	20	50
Saturday	45	15	60
Sunday	10	10	20

Table 9.2   Customers by day

Here it's better to use a spreadsheet – it's a 'stacked vertical bar chart'. You can use colour too if you have a colour printer, otherwise the different categories will show in shades of grey.

▶▶ ACTIVITY ═══════════════════════════════

If you have access to a spreadsheet, try doing the above table in a bar-chart format. If you type in the information exactly as above you can then use that for your source data for Chart Wizard (or similar in non-Excel spreadsheets). See how much more interesting it looks.

If you can do this over a period of weeks and see some real trends then you may be able to use it to decide how you approach the problem of bookings.

Line charts

These can also be used, as well as for break-even, for displaying sales levels by day or by month. You could use different lines for different departments, or compare year-to-year for a meeting presentation. You could also use them to show staffing levels in different months. Trying to describe these can be difficult – a picture (that is, chart) is far more effective.

▶▶ ACTIVITY ═══════════════════════════════

Using the Total Customers data only from the table above, practise doing a line chart.

More practise on spreadsheets

This exercise practises a range of techniques. Set up a spreadsheet for your own personal cash flow. Write down all your money coming in and going out, then try and set up a spreadsheet in the style of the cash forecast that was covered in Chapter 6. You could also draw a chart to show the surplus or deficit – what sort of chart would be good for this?

Here's the sort of things you might need:

Cash in	Cash out
Wages (net)	Rent or mortgage
Rent from lodger	Food
	Travel to work
	Household bills
	Clothes
	Entertainment
	Savings for holiday

Don't forget you'll also need to know what you have in the bank already.

Summary

In this chapter we have looked at how we can use spreadsheets for management tasks and discussed a range of techniques to improve our skills. You have:

▷ Discussed a range of design techniques to assist in the effective construction of a spreadsheet

▷ Practised exercises to aid in the development of skills

▷ Discussed a range of scenarios where spreadsheets might be used

▷ Discussed the use of charts to aid in decision making

▷ Practised chart construction by spreadsheet and by hand.

Quiz

1. The Number One Rule with all work is…

2. Why is spreadsheet design important?

3. Why should I bother learning about charts?

10

Being part of a company

▼
▼
▼
▼
▼

Introduction

Some of you may work in a very small business, where you know the owner and everybody else in the organization. The majority of the businesses in hospitality are small – pubs, restaurants, cafes, visitor attractions and so on.

But for others, you may feel that you are a very small part of a very large organization. Some hospitality companies are enormous – and may well be part of an even larger conglomerate (a multi-industry, multi-national corporation). We won't 'name names' here because businesses change ownership frequently and by the time you read this the information will be out of date. Some of the big names of five years ago are no longer around in the same way, and other previously small names are now big ones.

Whatever the size of the business, you *do* count, and in this chapter we want to show you how you fit into the larger organization, whether for now or for the future. We will look at the types of ownership and then the structure of companies and the type of accounts that they do. Later on we will consider two other ways that businesses can operate – under franchise and by management contract – where the building is owned by one entity but run by another.

By the end of this chapter, therefore, you should be able to:

▷   Distinguish between the different types of company ownership

▷   Describe the basic format of a company report

▷   Describe the differences between a franchise and a management contract.

Ownership of business

There are three basic types of ownership – sole trader, partnership and limited company. We will look at each in turn, describe the features and then look at the type of reports they have to produce by law. For the sole trader and partnership these are fairly simple but limited companies (which are generally much larger) have complex reports to produce.

Sole trader

This is one person in business who owns a pub, café, shop or similar and probably employs staff to work for them. Maybe you work for one of these. Legally the owner is fully responsible for all the activities of the business – and all the profits or losses. So, if the business fails, they are personally liable for the debts. It's not unusual, therefore, for the sole trader to have very few personal assets – the house, car, personal bank account and so on may all be held in their spouse or partner's name. This may sound rather unethical, but it is legal.

Sole traders do all their own business accounts, which they do need to keep separate from their personal accounts, and then pay income tax on any profits. They have to keep records but these can be fairly simple – records of all revenue and expenditure – and so a simple profit and loss (P&L) and balance sheet (BS) are adequate. One extra item you may see on the balance sheet in the 'financed by' section is 'drawings' which are monies taken out of the business by the owner as profits. These are shown separately to ensure that too much money isn't being extracted when the business can't afford it.

It's advisable to have the accounts formally reviewed by a chartered accountant once a year as they can help reduce the tax, and the Inland Revenue are less likely to query things if the accounts have been checked.

So, there are advantages and disadvantages of sole trader status:

For

▷ Simple accounts

▷ Keep the business under your own control

▷ Keep it small and manageable

▷ Plenty of time to pay tax

Against

▷ Lack of opportunity to expand as you're limited by your own funds (and any the bank will lend you)

▷ Personally liable for debts

Partnership

In a partnership two or more people go into business together. They don't have to be equal partners – one can own a greater percentage then the other(s). Often the percentage ownership is based on the amount of capital (initial money) invested in the business at the beginning, but this isn't always true. For instance, parents may invest in a pub which their children they run – but all remain equal partners. One invests money, the other skills and time. There can be some very big partnerships although generally you are not allowed to have more than 20. The majority of hospitality, tourism and leisure businesses are small and are owned and run by either a partnership or sole trader.

Legally they are all responsible for the running of the business – and so for profits or losses. Any profits are shared out according to the Partnership Agreement that, by law, they all have to sign (this contract also includes lots of other items such as what to do if they fall out, or decide to close the business). If the business fails then they are personally liable for the losses.

The way in which they prepare their accounts is a little more complicated than for a sole trader. Once the P&L has been calculated down to the Net profit line then an extra section is added – the appropriation account. This is where the profits are 'appropriated' (allocated, or portioned out) to the partners. The partners pay tax on their part of the profits.

If the partners shared profits equally then the Appropriation Account would look like this:

Net profit		£2,000
Appropriated:		
Partner 1	50%	£1,000
Partner 2	50%	£1,000

The BS has subsections in the 'Financed By' section which shows each partner's capital account and current account where their shares of the initial investment and profits are held. Again this is obviously a simple generalisation – an accountant is best qualified to advise you properly here.

Tax-wise, each partner is responsible for the tax on their own share of the business. So, the advantages and disadvantages of partnership status are:

For

▷   Fairly simple accounts

▷   Keep the business under control of the partners but with additional expertise from each partner

▷   Easier to expand if you all want to

Against

▷　　Still personally liable for debts

▷　　Sharing the business means sharing profits, but also losses

▷　　Potential for disagreement

Limited liability companies

This is the way that you reduce your liability for the debts of the company – while still sharing in the profits. Companies can be very small – or multinational giants. There are two types of limited company – private and public. If you invest in one of these your financial liability is limited to the amount you originally put in – you are not personally liable for the debts of the company.

The capital of the company (what was the 'Financed By' section before) is divided – or *shared* – out into millions (usually) of small, equal portions called shares. The way that you own part of the company is to own a proportion of the shares, of which more detail later. However, you as an individual may only be able to influence the management of the company if you are a director or very senior executive.

LTDs and LLPs

Private limited companies (usually abbreviated to Ltd) have shares that can be only owned by a restricted band of people – usually the original family owners and employees of the company. Ltd's often emerge from partnerships, when the owners decide that they want to keep the business separate from their personal affairs and reduce their financial liability in the case of loss.

There's a new form of Ltd called a Limited Liability Partnership (LLP) which is run like a partnership but has a separate legal entity and so has limited liability for debts. As these are only just coming into law in 2001 then it's impossible to predict how successful they'll be.

PLCs

Public limited companies (PLCs) have shares that can be bought and sold by anybody via the Stock Exchange (there's a bit more about the Stock Market further on in this chapter).

The advantages and disadvantages of a business being part of a company are:

For

     ▷   Shareholder's liability for debt is limited to the amount they invest

     ▷   Opportunity to raise funds from lots of sources

     ▷   Lots of expertise available from a range of people

     ▷   Easier to expand if the directors wish to

Against

     ▷   Complex accounts

     ▷   Lack of control by individuals

     ▷   Have to share the profits

We will go through the format of their accounts after we have considered how you might fit into the structure of a company. First, Figure 10.1 shows a simplified flow chart for a contract catering division to illustrate how the whole company is structured, from individual unit (where you might work) to the total corporation.

Figure 10.1   Company structure

The divisions or sections themselves may be registered as individual companies, usually wholly or substantially owned by the parent company, for tax or operational reasons.

Do you know which type of business you belong to? If it's a large one do you know what all the other divisions do?

Types of company accounts

As mentioned in Chapter 2, businesses have two types of accounts – management accounts and published accounts.

Management accounts are those that are used within the business and utilize the P&L and BS structures that we've used in earlier chapters. These are designed for the managers to help them run the business more effectively. You'll normally have one set of management accounts for each unit, and a summary for the overall business.

Published accounts are a legal requirement for limited companies and they are also designed for the owners of the company (known as shareholders), the investors and any other stakeholders – people who have an interest in how the company operates. This could include you!

The structure is formally specified so that all published accounts look the same. They are contained in the Annual Report, a glossy publication that also includes various other statements and statistics for the financial year. There are also interim reports that are a brief summary of the half-yearly results.

▶▶ ACTIVITY

Please try and obtain a copy of a company report. If you are employed by a PLC then try and get hold of one of theirs, otherwise a company in which you own shares or are interested in. Look at the content. Getting hold of a company report can take a bit of time. Sources are:

▶   Your Controller or Finance Director (if you have one)

▶   If you own shares you should be sent one automatically

▶   Write to (or telephone) the company Head Office and ask for one – they are legally obliged to send you one

▶   Go to the company web-site and see if it's there although sometimes some of the detail is omitted. Otherwise you should be able to e-mail an order through

▶   Order one via one of the web-based ordering services (such as ft.com).

Now let's 'walk through' a typical annual report and see what's in it.

Content of the Annual Report

Chairman (or Chief Executive Officer) statement

This tends to be as glossy as the report style! They obviously try to make the company look as good as possible, so if it's been a bad year they'll talk about 'challenges' and how things are improving. You need to study the contents of the entire report to see how open they've been about what has happened.

A good CEO or chairman will also thank the employees for their contribution to the company success. You'll often also read about the company's attitude towards environmental issues (sometimes in a separate statement).

Finance Director's statement

This focuses specifically on the financial performance of the company and will include some key ratios.

List of directors

This usually has a brief profile of who they are.

Directors emoluments

This is what they have been paid – and not just in money but also in share options, bonuses and benefits (the whole package can be ENORMOUS)

Profit and Loss statement

This is shown further on and is a little different from the structure we're used to. You'll also see a number in a column (often in italics) – this relates to the 'notes to the accounts' where you'll find lots of detail as to what makes up the particular line. You will see two years' figures – the immediate past year and the one before that. You may also see a summary statement for five years.

Balance sheet

Again, this is a bit different in layout and also has two years' figures.

Cash flow

This shows where the money has come from and gone to. It details all revenues, not just from sales but also from investments and interest payments. Some cash is tied up in stocks and debtors, other goes out to pay shareholders their profits (dividends) and to pay debts.

If you want to read more about the Cash Flow statement then see the reading list at the end of the chapter.

Notes to the Accounts

These are *really* useful because they contain lots of information about the company (such as number of employees, major shareholders, debts and so on) that's can't be shown on the P&L and BS. The number on the note is the reference number from the P&L or BS.

Why reports are useful to you

They can tell you a lot about the company. By carefully reading all the detail, and perhaps looking at a few ratios (more below), you can find out what their attitudes are and how successful they are in their various enterprises. What you might want to look at:

▷ Look at the turnover (revenue). How does it compare to previous years? Arc they doing better or worse?

▷ Look at profits. Are they growing? Think about why that would be. It can be good or bad depending on your viewpoint.

▷ Look at staffing costs and average wage costs (low wages might = high profits). Does the company talk about investing in its workforce? Do they pay pensions and offer training and development?

▷ Look at the directors' salaries – are they worth it? How does this compare to the average wage cost?

▷ Is the company growing in size, and hopefully without too much growth of debts?

▷ How do they stand on ethical issues? Do they invest in environmentally sound projects?

▷ Are they investing for the future – in staff, in equipment, in technology?

▷ Who owns the company?

▷ Is ownership in the hands of a few large stockholders?

▶▶ **ACTIVITY** ━━━━━━━━━━━━━━━━━━━━━━━━

Suppose your business was bought by another company who don't have a good environmental record? Or perhaps they've been 'outed' for unethical practices, or employing child labour in a Third World country. How do you react?

Published Profit and Loss report

This is the one found in the annual report.

To the right you'll see columns for the two years' trading and also the reference number for the Notes to the Accounts. Here is a very simplified explanation of the layout as there can be further data relating to other businesses that form part of the company.

Turnover (continuing operations) Revenue received from day-to-day trading

Less cost of sales This isn't the same as you are used to. It means ALL costs except administrative and selling costs

= *Gross profit* So this isn't the same as the GP on a P&L either

Less net operating expenses The selling and admin expenses
= *Operating profit*

Plus or minus profit/loss on sale If you sell a property or other fixed asset you may make a loss or profit of property and other fixed assets
= *Profit before interest*

Less net interest payable Interest on loans that you have to pay
= *Profit before taxation*

Less tax on profit from ordinary activities The corporation tax payable on these profits
= *Profit after taxation*

Less dividends paid This is the way that profits are shared out amongst the shareholders – see below when we discuss types of shares
= *Retained profit* This is money kept back by company for re-investment in the business

▶▶ **ACTIVITY** ▬▬▬▬▬▬▬▬▬▬▬▬▬▬▬▬▬▬▬▬▬▬▬▬▬▬

You could compare this to the annual report that you have and see what it contains. The Notes will help you decipher the various entries. Are there other items that appear? Do you know what they all mean? If necessary find a textbook (see the reading list) and look up the terminology. If you see a column headed 'exceptional items' then it's likely that the company bought or sold a substantial section of business. By showing these separately the reader can make comparisons to other years, and other investments.

Published balance sheet

Fixed assets

Tangible – Things you can touch – buildings, equipment and so on

Investments – Money invested in other companies, which is long-term and unlikely to change daily

Plus current assets

Stocks – These are all the same as an internal BS that you are familiar with
Debtors
Bank
Prepayments

Less creditors due within one year

Interest payable – These are all short-term (current) liabilities
Tax payable
Dividend payable
Creditors due within one year
Accruals

= Net current assets

Less: Creditors due after one year (also called 'debt') – other debts due for repayment over a year and include debentures which are a form of loan

= Total net assets

This is the balancing (total) figure

Shareholders fund (also called 'equity')

These are the monies that belong to the shareholders

Called-up share capital – The original value of the shares (NOT what's being quoted on the stock market)

Reserves – Money put aside for refurbishment in the future and also retained for future expansion

Profit and Loss account – Profits earned by the company that belong to the owners – the shareholders

=Total capital and reserves

The other balancing figure

▶▶ **ACTIVITY** ══════════════════════════════════

Again, look at 'your' report and see what's in it.

═══

Shares

The capital of a company is divided into lots of equal shares (their 'nominal value') which are then sold to the general public (and to banks, pension funds, investment trusts and other large investors). As a shareholder you are paid your proportion of the profits in the form of a dividend.

There are two main types of shares – *preference* and *ordinary*.

Preference shares

The reason that they are 'preferred' is because:

▷   The dividend is paid first

▷   In the event of liquidation, the preference shareholders are repaid before other shareholders.

These shares carry a fixed rate of dividend which is expressed as a percentage of the nominal value so, for instance, a £1 (nominal value) 9% preference shares would earn 9 pence dividend per year. This payment doesn't change whether it is a good year or not.

Ordinary shares

The ordinary shareholders bear the greatest risk because

▷   Their dividend is only paid when there are enough profits, although if profits are good then they may earn high dividends

▷   They are last in line for repayment if the company fails (after *everybody* else).

Dividends are paid in 'pence per share'.

How to calculate dividends:

Preference shares are paid in two parts and are called *interim* (half-year) and *final* (year-end).

Example: 9% preference share dividend for 1,000 £1 shares

Interim	4.5% x £1	4.5 pence	x 1,000	= £45
Final	4.5% x £1	4.5 pence	x 1,000	= £45
			Total paid	= £90

Ordinary shares earn a different amount according to the profits available.

Example: £1 shares – half year profits good so interim dividend high at 10p/ share. Final profits less good so dividend lower at 6p/share, for 1,000 shares

Interim	10 pence	x 1,000	= £100
Final	6 pence	x 1,000	= £60
		Total paid	= £160

Ratios that can be calculated

In addition to the ratios that we've covered in other chapters there are a few that you can do on published accounts too. Some of these will be stated in the annual report, others you'll need to work out yourself.

They can help you understand more about how the company is performing. Remember, though, that what's a 'good' ratio for one person may be 'bad' for another. For instance, a high profit percentage may be good for shareholders (more dividends) but mean a lower wage percentage (bad for employees) although usually it is good for both for a successful company can, in theory, afford to pay higher rates. Employees may also benefit from company share options, which can be a profitable way for staff to have a financial interest in their company without having to find cash to invest by themselves.

$$\text{Return on ordinary shareholders' funds} = \frac{\text{Profit after tax and preference share dividend}}{\text{Ordinary shareholders' funds}} \%$$

This is the percentage return that ordinary shareholders may see from profits. It isn't the same as dividends because it's calculated before reserves.

$$\text{Return on capital employed (ROCE)} = \frac{\text{Profit before interest \& tax}}{\text{Shareholders' funds + long-term debt}} \%$$

The capital employed is the debt and equity together – so all the long term liabilities. ROCE means the percentage profit compared to these long-term liabilities.

$$\text{Earnings per share (in pence) (EPS)} = \frac{\text{Profit after tax \& preference share dividend}}{\text{Number of issued ordinary shares}}$$

This is how much profit is earned on average by each share. It's not the actual dividend figure because it's calculated before reserves are extracted.

$$\text{Price/earnings ratio (P/E)} = \frac{\text{Market price per share}}{\text{Earnings per share}}$$

We've talked about the 'nominal value' of the share before, but they can be bought and sold on the stock market at whatever price people are willing to pay. The price is based on predictions of profits (and hence dividends) and the growth of the company so – the higher the market price, the more desirable they are. The P/E ratio measures the market price against the EPS.

$$\text{Gearing} = \frac{\text{Long term loans + preference shares + short term debt}}{\text{Ordinary shares \& reserves}}$$

Gearing is the relationship between debt (money borrowed) to equity (shareholders' funds). Generally, the lower the gearing (less debt to equity) then the more stable the company is. A company that is 'highly geared' has borrowed a lot of money to expand, which isn't a problem for as long as the lending institutions (banks etc.) still trust you. If the trust is destroyed then the banks may 'call in' their debts which can often mean the collapse of the company.

Here is an example of gearing:

Two Companies – Alpha and Beta

	Alpha (£000)	Beta (£000)
Issued share capital		
50p Ordinary shares	300	450
10% Preference shares	225	
Reserves		
Renewal reserve	105	150
Retained earnings	225	300
Loan capital		
8% debentures	450	
10% debentures		225

(Note that debentures are a type of loan)

Calculation of gearing

(Formula is total debt divided by total equity expressed as a percentage)

	Alpha	Beta
Sources	$\frac{450+225}{300+105+225}$	$\frac{225}{450+150+300}$
=	$\frac{675}{630}$	$\frac{225}{900}$
=	107%	25%

Alpha has a very high gearing and so is vulnerable if the banks and other lending institutions were to lose confidence.

Beta has very low gearing and could (and should) borrow money for expansion if they have a profitable product or service for which there is a thriving market. Here's a small exercise for you to calculate some ratios, based on the above and any others that you can remember that have already been covered.

PROFIT & LOSS ACCOUNT

Trading	£000s
Turnover	1,875
- Cost of sales	(1,410)
= Gross profit	465
- Operating expenses	(190)
= Profit before interest	275
- Interest	(25)
= Profit before tax	250
- Tax	(82)
= Profit after tax	168
Dividends	(100)
= Retained profit for year	68

BALANCE SHEET

Fixed assets		
Tangible		510
Current assets		
Stocks	375	
Debtors	250	
Cash & short-term deposits	60	
Total	685	
Creditors within one year		
Bank and other borrowings	(437)	
Net current assets	248	
Total assets less current liabilities		758
Creditors due after one year		
Bank and other borrowings		(340)
= Net assets employed		418
Capital & reserves		
Called up share capital		250
Profit & Loss account (profit after tax)		168
Equity shareholders' funds		418

Assume that the market price per share is £1.50, and that there are 500,000 shares. You are asked to calculate appropriate ratios (don't forget there are others we did in earlier chapters too).

▼
▼

TIP

Work out the nominal (issue) price of the shares first by taking the issued share capital divided by the number of shares.

Here's the answer:

Ordinary shares	Share capital	£250,000	
	Number or ordinary shares	500,000	
	So the nominal price of each is	£0.50	
Return on Capital Employed	Profit before interest and tax	£275,000	65.8%
	Net Assets	£418,000	
Gross Profit	Gross profit	£465,000	24.8%
	Sales	£1,875,000	
Profitability	Profit before interest and tax	£275,000	14.7%
	Sales	£1,875,000	
Gearing	Debt	£340,000	81.3%
	Equity	£418,000	
Liquidity – Current ratio	Current assets	£685,000	1.57 :1
	Current liabilities	£437,000	
Liquidity – Acid test	Debtors + cash	£310,000	0.71 :1
	Current liabilities	£437,000	
Earnings per share	Profit after tax	£168,000	£0.34
	No. issued ordinary shares	500,000	
Dividend per share	Ordinary dividend paid	£100,000	£0.20
	No. issued ordinary shares	500,000	
Price earnings ratio	Market price per share	£1.50	4.46 :1
	Earnings per share	£0.34	
Debtor days	Debtors	£250,000	48.67 days
	Average sales per day	£5,137	

▶▶ **ACTIVITY**

Are these results good or bad? Think about what these numbers are telling you. Then get a copy of a quality newspaper ('broadsheet' not tabloid) and go to the financial pages. Look at the prices quoted for various companies – it doesn't have to be hospitality. Then look at some of the comments made in other sections.

Share ownership

Existing companies

These are already quoted on the Stock Exchange. There are two prices quoted – BUY and SELL. Transactions are made through 'brokers' who will obtain the best market price that they can, and take a commission on the sale. Once sold the actual transfer of shares and cash takes place five days after sale is made. Anybody over 18 with the cash can do it!

A *bull* market is optimistic, generally where there are more investors wanting to purchase shares than there are willing sellers, because of a positive outlook for company performance and profitability.

A *bear* market is pessimistic, generally there are more investors wanting to sell shares than there are purchasers, because of a negative outlook on company performance and profitability.

New companies

If you want to buy shares in a brand new company that hasn't yet been trading on the stock market (although they will probably have been in business as an Ltd or partnership for some time) then you will see an 'Offer for Sale' when they 'go public'. You apply to buy a certain number of shares. Depending on how well-subscribed they are (that is, how popular) you may or may not get all the shares you ask for.

Although shares are issued at their *nominal* (or face) value you will probably have to pay a *premium* which is an additional amount. The higher the potential demand for shares, the higher the premium. For instance, two companies going public each with £1 (nominal) shares to offer:

▷   Company A is profitable, innovative and has identified a niche market and so potentially will make large profits.

Its £1 shares are offered at £3.50 (a premium of £2.50) which reflects the demand and potential profits.

▷   Company B is also profitable (otherwise it wouldn't be going public) but isn't as fashionable as Company A, and so the future predictions aren't as good.

Its £1 shares are offered at £1.50 (a premium of only £0.50) which reflects the reduced demand.

Franchising and management contracts

Many companies both own and operate properties under their own name. However, sometimes they wish either to use a well-known brand name or to just operate with another company owning the property. One approach is franchising and another is management contracting and the two are fairly similar in concept although with different modes of operation.

Franchising

Franchising occurs when an owner (usually of property but sometimes just of skills) decides to go into business and use the expertise of an established operator. Typically this will be an established brand name with a standard product. This is one of the few ways that a small operator can enter the larger market. They take on a licence for a particular area.

Examples of franchises in hospitality are pizza restaurants, fast-food take-aways and hotel groups. A hotel group looking to franchise will typically have many hotels that they wish to operate under their own control but with a proven brand name. The operator stays in control – it is *their* business.

Advantages of taking on a franchise are:

▷   Availability of a new market with a proven brand name

▷   Assistance in finding a site, and exclusive trading within a given area (so the franchiser won't grant any more licences within your 'patch')

▷   Assistance in planning the layout of the property (if used – you can franchise a window cleaning business, for instance)

▷   Advice on all aspects of the business

▷   Training of core management staff

▷   Menus and recipes if required

▷   Supplies of branded products (book matches, paper napkins, etc.)

▷   Advertising and promotion on a national level.

Advantages to the franchiser (the owner of the brand) are:

▷   The opportunity to expand their business with little capital.

▷   The opportunity to receive a fee or 'royalty' of a percentage of the sales, plus often a set fee for the other services

▷ Exposure in a much wider market (it's called 'market penetration')

▷ The ability to keep their own core operation (head office) compact whilst still providing extensive services.

There are also benefits to the customer as they see a proven brand name but with the comfort of having an operator who knows the local market and hence local needs. The only disadvantage to franchisors and franchisees is the dependence on each other and hence potential for problems if either fails to keep their side of the agreement.

Management contracts

These are used where the owner of the brand wishes to continue to operate and expand their name and business without a major capital investment. Typically a property company will own the actual building but they are not interested in running the business themselves (unlike a franchise). They will ask someone else to do it for them by hiring a management company to run the business with their established name. This is most common in hotels – many of the major international groups operate in this way.

The advantages to the operator are:

▷ Expansion (often globally) of the brand – again it's market penetration

▷ A large number of properties where managers can be placed and then train the local workforce in the company standards

▷ As a result improved (international ?) career opportunities for staff

▷ Receipt of fees, often based on a percentage of sales but more recently on a percentage of profits

▷ The ability to influence local trade without major financial investment

▷ The owner provides funds for all capital investment and for working capital, so there is limited financial outlay

▷ A fixed time period for operation – often five years now.

The advantages to the owner of the property are:

▷ The benefit of a known brand

▷ The benefit of trained management and standardized systems

▷ A guarantee of maintenance of standards

▷   An income with minimal effort although with major investment (they provide the building, fixtures and fittings, equipment and working capital)

▷   Standard reporting of profits using the Uniform System of Accounts (see Chapter 2) for consistency.

There have been several examples where hotel groups have entered into joint ventures to own properties with other partners, often in countries with a previous lack of investment and/or hotel infrastructure. For instance, in some Eastern European countries major groups linked up with local property owners and governments as joint partners. Here the lack of investment for decades coupled with a growing market created the opportunity for development. The initial investment by the management company guarantees their interest and commitment to making the contract work (they're not going to pull out after a year if the business is unsuccessful). Typically after several years as joint owners the hotel group will sell out to the other partners or to commercial investors, but continue to manage the property on an ongoing basis.

One other area where the management contract approach has been used is for hotels or restaurants in receivership. The property will then be 'owned' by a bank or financial institution as a result of the original owners going bankrupt. As a going concern the business is more likely to be sold and also less likely to deteriorate so the new owner may well want to keep the business running. In this case a small management contractor (perhaps even a management consultant) may be asked to operate the business, usually without a standard brand name and for a limited period of time.

Summary

In this chapter we have reviewed the structure of companies and hopefully helped you to visualize where you might fit as part of the 'bigger picture'. We've looked at the structure of annual reports and identified some ratios that can be used to analyse these. The later part of the chapter described franchises and management contracts. Hence you are now able to:

▷   Identify the differences between the three types of business ownership – sole trader, partnership and limited company

▷   Describe the main features of an annual report

▷   Analyse ratios relevant to published accounts

▷   Identify the differences between management contracts and franchises.

Quiz

1. How many people are involved in a partnership?

2. What's your financial liability if you are a sole trader?

3. What does 'return on equity' mean?

4. Is the chairman's statement relevant to the annual report?

5. If a hotel group owns and operates a business is this likely to be a franchise or a management contract?

Developing your skills

▼
▼
▼
▼
▼

Anticipating trends ◀

Developing your financial skills further ◀

Looking after your staff ◀

Introduction

In this chapter we will look at using this information to help you develop further as a manager and consider how to look ahead, not just by forecasting but by predicting trends and so identifying how you can best use this to your advantage.

By improving your own skills as a manager, in the future you will be well equipped to take advantage of all the opportunities available to you. This will include looking at the types of training and education that you can undertake, and other areas that might be useful. Although professional development may not be immediately obvious as a finance topic it's relevant to all of us – and financial management *is* a key skill for all hospitality managers now.

By the end of this chapter you will be able to:

▷   Collate the various themes of this book

▷   Be aware of trends in the industry

▷   Describe some of the education and training opportunities available.

Key themes

So, what have you learned from this book?

▷   The importance of maximising revenue in order to optimise profits or achieve BEP. A combination of control, accurate pricing and marketing is needed, and ratios are invaluable in helping identify areas for action.

▷   The importance of controlling costs and stocks without affecting customer service – so you need to optimise rather than minimize these. Different types of costs are found in different sectors, and in fact some units or departments have only costs and not revenues. Where there are very tight margins the control of costs is paramount to achieve business objectives – small variances, and small actions (such as the slice of tomato) can make big differences overall. Being able to identify where the differences are by using ratios and standard costing techniques is essential to profitability (or BEP).

▷   Attitudes of managers are crucial. If you 'lead from the top' and make it clear that wastage and theft are unacceptable then half the battle is won. Most staff are intrinsically honest, but sloppy and/or dishonest leadership can make them careless too. Walking the job ('MBWA') is one of the best ways to identify problems, especially when used in conjunction with ratio analysis.

▷ Planning all aspects of the business helps managers in a variety of ways. Forecasting customer levels and use of standard costing techniques allows planning of purchasing and staffing which minimizes wastage and hence costs. Planning the control of all areas helps you anticipate potential problems before they occur and the use of spreadsheets is vital in achieving accurate results.

▷ Cash and stocks are very desirable and so need strong controls at all stages of the working capital cycle. Forecasting cash requirements is helpful to the business, but nothing beats simple effective systems and a good lock with minimal distribution of keys.

▷ Decisions made at unit level impact at higher levels of the organization. Some management reports are designed for use by managers within their own areas, others for the general manager or owner. If you are part of a larger organization then your unit report will be amalgamated with others to produce overall company reports. These are then converted into a different structure for publication in an annual report that addresses the needs of the various stakeholders.

▷ The customer always comes first.

Anticipating trends

A key to your successful career in the future will be your ability to forecast trends. You may think you are a small fish in a big pond, but hopefully you'll grow into a bigger fish (which may be one reason why you are reading this).

We've been looking at your current operation, mostly from a short-term perspective. It's important, though, to also look strategically – a long way ahead. You need to try and anticipate how the business will grow, and then whether you will be a part of that. Many of the techniques we've learned can help you because by tracking what has happened you can make some predictions for the future.

For instance, if you see that revenues are growing and the company is buying more businesses, then the chances are that your career will grow too. On the other hand, if the business is struggling then you might want to start considering your next career move. Below are some things to look out for. You should remember that, although these examples don't appear to be directly financial in nature, all activities have a financial impact on the business in one way or another.

▷   Growth in hospitality and tourism as a whole

▷   Changes in the national economy which affect visitors from overseas

▷   Incidents or events that affect tourism (and hence most hospitality businesses) – such as foot and mouth disease or major sporting events

▷   Trends in eating out

▷   Trends in regional and local business, such as new hotels, hospitals, visitor attractions

▷   Anything happening in your sector

▷   Anything happening in your company or organization.

How do you find these out? – by reading (see below), listening, watching, going to places and general participation in the activities of your operation and the industry (and perhaps your professional association too). There also some web-sites listed at the back of the book.

Developing your financial skills further

Now that you have reviewed what you have learned, what next? Practise!

Hopefully having worked your way through this book you'll have been able to learn new techniques and practise a range of skills. You can use them in the workplace in all sorts of ways to really help you become a better supervisor or manager. It obviously depends on how much financial information is available to you – the attitude of senior managers can vary – but by being proactive you'll be able to make progress to a real understanding of the financial relevance of what you do.

Here are some suggestions:

▷   If you have financial statements then ask to see them each month. Look at the actual against budget for both revenues and costs, and see if you can identify what's working well and what isn't. Can you identify why things have happened? If it's good you could do it again, if it isn't so good, can you fix it?

▷ You could calculate ratios if they're not already done. Is there a relationship between volume and price? If sales have fallen, have costs fallen too? Which costs are fixed, and which are variable?

▷ Next time something needs pricing, or costing, could you help?

▷ Compare a budgeted recipe cost to the actual. Are there any variances and, if so, why?

▷ Do a forecast of customers, and see how it impacts on other areas.

▷ Look at other businesses as a customer yourself, and learn from them – both what they are doing well and what they're falling behind on. Sometimes you can be more objective looking at an operation that isn't your own, where you don't know the people or the quirks of the operation (and so don't make excuses for them).

Reading

Magazines and journals

Trade magazines are one of the best ways to keep up to date because they talk about what's happening now. They do report on day-to-day activities and there will be one at least (and probably more) that focus on your sector. The professional associations all have their own journals or newsletters too. You get a lot of opinions in the trade press and not everybody agrees with these!

Books (like this one)

At the end of each chapter there has been a range of suitable books quoted, but there are a lot more. This is just a personal selection that matches with the topics we've discussed but you may well find many others that you prefer. In addition to the books in each chapter there is some general reading at the end of this one that may be helpful too.

Using books can be a major help in developing your skills, so if you don't get on with a particular writer please try others. Different books suit different people – some people like a very technical style, others prefer a more user-friendly approach – it's all a matter of taste. If you aren't technically minded then books written for non-specialists may be best for you – for example if you want more on finance then a book titled 'finance for non-financial managers' or similar will be written in a non-expert style.

Where to find these

When you've decided the sort of information that you want to find out then it's a case of going to look at what's available.

University and college libraries

They will usually let you go in and look at books ('for reference') although you won't be able to borrow them unless you are a registered student. It's worth checking first, though, that they do offer hospitality courses. The more courses they offer (and the higher the level) the greater the range of books, journals and trade magazines they are likely to have.

Local libraries

The range of hospitality books will be minimal (if any) so you need to look at the business studies areas. They tend to stock 'beginner-level' books which assume that you are 'intelligent but uninformed' (which you are, of course!). Local libraries are excellent for careers and education information, both local and national. You can also usually access the Internet from a library although you may need to book first and pay a fee.

HCIMA

They have a library that you can go and visit if you are a member. It's worth checking what they have in a particular topic area before you go, though. They will also send you things by mail although return postage can be expensive.

Bookshops

Academic bookshops stock a reasonable range of books and can order for you if you wish. You can always go in and 'thumb the shelves' although again their range may be limited if they are not a hospitality specialist. Ordinary bookshops tend to just have general business-type books.

Online

If you go into some of the Internet bookshops you may be able to look at the (limited) descriptions of books that are available. Alternatively, why not find the names of some publishers (the reading lists in this book give you a start) and look at their web-sites. You may be able to buy direct.

Financial skills

Have you 'got the bug'? If you enjoy finance then you may want to develop your skills in this area a bit more (or lots more).

If you just want to be more financially competent then reading more in the area will help – and there's been a list of books in each chapter to help. There are also a few more general texts at the end of this chapter to help you. You can also study short courses locally – see below for some suggestions.

If you really think you like numbers – and as we've seen it's a lot about logic and being able to use a calculator, rather than an ability to do mathematics – then you could consider more formal financial training. The British Association of Hospitality Accountants (BAHA – see the web-site address) runs courses for people wishing to develop their skills. Their qualifications give you some exemptions from CIMA (Chartered Institute of Management Accountants) examinations, which are the more formal accounting qualifications probably best suited for practising financial managers.

BAHA is also a good source of information about hospitality financial management issues and also holds meetings both regionally and in London, where you can meet with other financial professionals from the industry. The HCIMA (Hotel and Catering International Management Association) has a similar approach and, being much larger, has frequent events within each local area.

Careers in finance

If you're good at numbers then think about working in an accounts office. You don't have to do all the accountancy exams if you don't want to, as there are lots of opportunities for people in different areas of control that don't require a lot of formal qualifications.

Training and education

You need to get as much as you can! It extends your skills, gives you perspective and helps you understand how other areas and people 'tick'. Although we're concentrating on finance this is important for other areas too. Training and education can be in-company or independent. You can often persuade employers to pay for development that is generally in your area of work although they are more likely to pay for short courses than long ones (such as a Master's course that is very expensive). You can borrow money to study though (see *Money to Learn* in the reading list).

Some educational courses earn you qualifications, others just develop your skills. Here are some ideas:

Local authority evening (or day) classes

These tend to run in school terms. You can study a wide range of skills, some that will result in qualifications, some not. You may have to do quite a bit of studying in your own time. There are some in hospitality, but any business-studies area would be useful too.

Certificate and diploma courses

These tend to be vocational – focusing on skills rather than management approaches. They are usually run in local further education colleges. You may be able to study full time, part time or at a distance. You may be able to study on day-release from work. Some professional associations (such as BAHA) run their own courses.

Degree courses

These are run by universities and some colleges. You may have to study full time, which would mean you concentrating on education for a few years, rather than work (though you may be able to work part time). You can usually get a grant to pay your fees but you still have to find a lot of extra cash to fund this. You may also be able to study at a distance or online.

Masters level

This is postgraduate level study. You don't necessarily need an undergraduate degree to study at this level as some universities have an open-entry approach which means that you can join providing you have sufficient management experience – usually two or three years. You'll find it tough at first, but the rewards can be enormous. Several universities now offer courses via on-line learning and there are lots of paper-based ones around too. Learning by yourself can be very lonely and time-consuming, so make sure it suits you before you sign up.

Anything to help your self-development is good – and that can mean non-hospitality things too. The important thing is that you learn and then promote that learning on your CV. So, for example, drama classes aren't just about having fun. They develop your self-confidence, your ability to speak in public, to think on your feet and to present to an audience.

Looking after your staff

Finally – one of the common themes about hospitality is that it is all about people. It's not just numbers – people are crucial to the industry both as customers and as employees. It makes sense, therefore, to look after them.

The main problems from a control aspect are theft and wastage and effective management of these is dependent on effective management of your customers and, most importantly, the staff who work with you. Accurate systems and physical controls are important but it is people who use these.

For you to be an effective manager means developing a culture of trust and integrity by leading from the top – if you are honest then they will be so too. If they are trusted to behave honestly and professionally then effective controls will happen and the result will be a profitable business.

Last, please recognize achievements – notice things that are working well as well as those that aren't. Praise is crucial to all of us, whether formal through appraisal or informal via a 'pat on the back'. Look after your staff and they'll make your job easier in return. A last mini-case for you:

Mini-case

The department had been enormously busy and the workload had been made worse as two staff were off – one on holiday and another on maternity leave.

Most staff had worked extra time to help out but weren't entitled to overtime payments. The manager could have made a case to pay everybody a small bonus, but they would have forgotten about it in a couple of days.

Instead she went out and bought each person a big box of very good chocolates as a present. This made an immediate difference to morale – the staff knew that she'd taken trouble to do this and that this meant she cared about them and recognized that they did a good job. Although they were all still tired they were able to see that the overload would soon be at an end.

This does show you that pay isn't the only motivator, or even the most effective – often it's how you behave and care about your staff that matters.

Appendix A : Reading list

Caterer & Hotelkeeper (every week!) and other trade press for your sector

HCIMA yearbook 2001

Anthony G, Fazal Z, and Sloper T, (1997) *Pubs and Restaurants: an Industry Accounting and Auditing Guide,* Accountancy Books Milton Keynes

Atrill P and McLaney E, (1999) *Financial Accounting for Non-Specialists,* 2nd edn., Prentice Hall, Hemel Hemstead

Baker S, Bradley P and Huyton J, (2000) *Principles of Hotel Front Office Operations,* Cassell, London

Braham B, (1993) *Hotel Front Office*, 2nd edn., Stanley Thornes, Cheltenham

Brett M, (2000) *How to Read the Financial Pages*, 5th edn., Random House Business Books, London

Brotherton B (ed.), (2000), *An introduction to the UK Hospitality Industry: A Comparative Approach*, Butterworth-Heinemann, Oxford

Bruning T, (1999) *Publicans Handbook* , 2nd edn., The Publican, London

Chin J, Barney W and O'Sullivan H, (1995) *Hotels: an Industry Accounting and Auditing Guide,* Accountancy Books, Milton Keynes

Coltman M and Jagels M, (2001), *Hospitality Management Accounting*, 7th edn., Van Nostrand Reinhold, New York

Cousins J, Foskett D and Shortt D, (1995) *Food & Beverage Management*, Longman, Harlow

Cracknell H, Kaumann R and Nobis G, (2000) *Practical Professional Catering Management,* 2nd edn., Macmillan, Basingstoke

Davis B, Lockwood A and Stone S, (1998) *Food and Beverage Management*, 3rd edn., Butterworth Heinemann, Oxford

Dittmer P and Griffin G, (1999) *Principles of Food, Beverage and Labor Cost Controls*, 6th edn., Van Nostrand Reinhold, New York

Dix C and Baird E, (1998) *Front Office Operations*, 4th edn., Addison Wesley Longman, Harlow

Drury C, (1998) *Costing – An Introduction*, 4th edn., International Thomson Business Press, London

East J, (1993) *Managing Quality in the Catering Industry,* Croner

Fewell A and Wells N, (1992) *Marketing,* Hospitality Managers' pocket books, Butterworth Heinemann, Oxford

Field H, (1995) 'Financial Management Implications of Hotel Management Contracts', *Accounting and Finance for the International Hospitality Industry*, Harris P (ed.), Butterworth Heinemann

Gee G, (1997) *Calculations for Hospitality and Catering*, 3rd edn., Hodder and Stoughton, London

Harris PJ, (1999) *Profit Planning*, 2nd edn., Hospitality Managers' pocket books, Butterworth Heinemann, Oxford

HCIMA Yearbook 2001, Hotel and Catering International Management Association

Hindle T, (1998) *Pocket International Business Terms*, Economist, London

International Association of Hospitality Accountants.(1996) *Uniform System of Accounts for the Lodging Industry* 9th edn., Hotel Association of New York City

Jenner S, (2000) *Graduate Career Handbook*, Financial Times/Prentice Hall

Johns N, (1996) *Productivity Management in Hospitality and Tourism*, Cassell, London

Jones C and Jewett V, (1998) *Managing Facilities*, Hospitality Managers' pocket books, Butterworth Heinemann, Oxford

Jones P and Merricks P, (1994) *The Management of Food Service Operations*, Cassell

Jones P and Pizam A, (1993) *The International Hospitality Industry*, Pitman Publishing, London

Knowles T, (1998) *Hospitality Management*, 2nd edn., Longman, Harlow

Kotas R, (1999) *Management Accounting for Hospitality and Tourism*, 3rd edn., International Thomson Business Press, London

Kotas R and Jayawardena C, (1994) *Profitable Food and Beverage Management*, Hodder & Stoughton, London

Laser Compendium of Higher Education, 2000, Butterworth Heinemann, Oxford

Lashley C and Morrison A, (2000) *In Search of Hospitality*, Butterworth Heinemann, Oxford

Lillicrap D, Cousins J and Smith R, (1998) *Food and Beverage Service*, 5th edn., Hodder & Stoughton, London

Medlik S and Ingram H, (2000) *The Business of Hotels*, 4th edn., Butterworth Heinemann, Oxford

Money to Learn -Financial Help for Adults in Further Education and Training, booklet from the Department for Education and Employment

NVQ/SVQ 2 (1993) *Catering and hospitality – Serving Food and Drink in the Restaurant – Student Guide*, Stanley Thornes

NVQ/SVQ 2 (1993) *Catering and Hospitality -Serving Food and Drink in the Bar – Student Guide,* Stanley Thornes

O'Connor C, (2000) *Hospitality Management a Strategic Approach*, Blackhall

O'Connor P, (2000) *Using Computers in Hospitality*, 2nd edn., Cassell, London

Owen G, (1998) *Accounting for Hospitality,* Tourism and Leisure, 2nd edn., Pitman, London

Parker K, (1999) *Buying and Running a Small Hotel,* 2nd edn., How to Books, Oxford

Pedler R, Burgoyne J and Boydell T, (2001) *A Managers Guide to Self-Development*, 4th edn., McGraw Hill

Perdue J, Montgomery R, Shock P and Stefanelli J, (1998) *A Club Manager's Guide to Private Parties and Club Function,* John Wiley, New York

Reid W and Myddelton DR, (2000) *The Meaning of Company Accounts,* 7th edn., Gower

Ridgway J and Ridgway B, (1994) *The Catering Management Handbook,* Kogan Page, London

Roberts J, (1993) *Marketing for the Hospitality Industry,* Hodder and Stoughtonm, London

Rushmore S, (1999) 'Structuring management contracts', *Hotels*, vol. 33, no. 5

Sackler W and Trapani S, (1996) *Food service cost control using Excel,* John Wiley, New York

Sargeant M and Lyle T, (1998) *Successful Pubs and Inns*, 2nd edn., Hospitality Managers' pocket books, Butterworth Heinemann, Oxford

Schmidgall, RS (1997) *Hospitality Industry Managerial Accounting,* 4th edn., Educational Institute of the American Hotel and Motel Association, East Lansing, Michigan

The Times A-Z of careers and jobs, (2000) 9th edn.,

TriHospitality, (2001) *United Kingdom Hotel Industry 2001,* TriHospitality Consulting, London

Waller K, (1996) *Improving Food and Beverage Performance,* Hospitality Managers' pocket books, Butterworth Heinemann, Oxford

Wood R, (1997) *Working in the Hospitality Industry,* Kogan Page

Wood R, (2000) *Strategic Questions in Food and Beverage Management,* Butterworth Heinemann, Oxford

Yeoman I and Ingold A, (1997) *Yield ManagementSstrategies for Service Industries,* International Thomson Business Press, London

Appendix B : Useful websites

abtanet.com
Association of British Travel Agents

accountingweb.com
Accounting information

acfws.org
Academy of Food and Wine

ahma.com
American Hotel and Motel Association

baha-uk.org.uk
British Association of Hospitality Accountants

bha-online.org.uk
British Hospitality Association

blra.co.uk
Breweries and Licensed Retailers Association

british-franchise.org
British Franchise Association

caterer.com
Caterer & Hotelkeeper magazine

chrie.org
Council for Hotel, Restaurant and Institutional Educators (US)

chme.co.uk
Council for Hospitality Management Education (UK)

cim.co.uk
Chartered Institute of Marketing

cimaglobal.uk
Chartered Institute of Management Accountants

cipd.co.uk
Chartered Institute of Personnel & Development

cips.co.uk
Chartered Institute of Purchasing and Supply

culture.gov.uk
Department of Culture, Media & Sport

dfes.gov.uk
Department of Education & Skills

dti.gov.uk
Department of Trade & Industry

edexcel.org.uk
ExExcel Foundation

fsb.org.uk
Federation of Small Businesses

ft.com
Financial Times – for financial data about hospitality

greenhotelier.com
Environmental hotel site

hcima.org.uk
HCIMA site

hftp.com
Hotel Financial & Technology Professionals

hitec.org
Hospitality industry technology association (US)

hospitalitynet.com
General hospitality site

hospitalitynet.org
General hospitality site

hotel-online.com
General hospitality site

htf.org.uk
Hospitality Training Foundation

ilam.org.uk
Institute of Leisure Amenity Management

laca.org.uk
Local Authority Caterers Organisation

meetings.ccm
Meetings Industry Association

ragb.org.uk
Restaurant Association of Great Britain

reuters.com
Reuters news agency

springboarduk.org.uk
Springboard – industry employment organisation

theaccu.co.uk
Association of Contract Catering Users

ukparks.com
British Holiday and Home Park Association

visabrc.com
Visa card

wiredhotelier.com
General hospitality site

Appendix C: Quizzes and answers

Chapter 2

1. *What goes in fixed assets?*
   Fixed Assets are items that the business **owns** that last a long time. Examples are buildings, fixtures and fittings, vehicles. Most of these are depreciated (see 4).

2. *What are current liabilities?*
   The are items that we OWE, and are repayable on a short-term basis. Examples are overdrafts, creditors (bills we still have to pay), accruals (see Answer 3, below).

3. *If your electricity bill is charged until 25th July, what happens to the 26-31st consumption?*
   You need to ACCRUE for these 'missing' 6 days in the July accounts. You should calculate the amount still unpaid and add it to Electricity category in the Utility department expenses. The accrual is reversed in August when the actual bill (including these 6 days, and part of August) is paid.

4. *If you had an oven costing £6,000 and estimated it would last 10 years, how much depreciation do you charge per year?*
   An oven is a fixed asset and so the £6,000 needs to be divided out amongst the years it will 'live'. The £6,000 divided by 10 years = £600 per year. If you have 12 periods per year then that is £50 each period. It would normally be expressed as 'depreciation at 10%'.

5. *What does GOP stand for?*
   Gross Operating Profit. It's the line that represents all the results from daily trading (revenue less expenses) and is the figure on which general managers' performance is usually measured. Below this line comes the Fixed Charges, which aren't controllable on a day-to-day basis.

6. *What's the best way to find the true Cost of Sales?*
   First, do a stocktake! This will give you an accurate figure of what you still hold in inventory. Then find out the purchases figure, the cost of transfer to staff meals and any other relevant data. You can then do the calculation.

Chapter 3

1. *What is revenue?*
   The sales made to customers for products and service received.

2. *What are the two main ways of identifying problems?*
    MBWA (Management By Walking About), ratios and other management information.

3. *Can you identify the main ways of increasing revenue?*
    Control and Marketing – adding customers and adding spend.

4. *How do you calculate occupancy?*
    Divide the number of spaces (rooms or seats) available by the number sold.

5. *How do you calculate average spend?*
    Divide the sales by the number of customers.

Chapter 4

1. *What's a variable cost?*
    It's a cost that changes with the level of business – if you sell something you incur a cost. Raw materials are the best example but there are many more.

2. *What's a fixed cost?*
    A cost that doesn't change much and can't easily be reduced. Their behaviour isn't related to the level of business. Examples are salaries, rent and depreciation.

3. *Why is it important to know the difference?*
    Because you can control variable costs easily but fixed costs are less manageable.

4. *What are the main ratios used for food and beverage cost?*
    Food and beverage cost percentages (and/ or gross profits) and average costs per customer.

5. *What's the most important cost in cleaning a hospital ward? Can you reduce this cost easily?*
    Payroll is by far the biggest cost. It's not easily controlled because in this environment you may well have a lot of long-serving employees and a standard area to clean each day – so the payroll is largely fixed.

6. *How do you calculate productivity?*
    See the range of ratios above – productivity is generally the amount of time it takes to do something. Different productivity ratios are applicable in different sectors.

Chapter 5

1. *How do you gross up?*
   Divide the cost price by the cost % to give the selling price – in other words, divide the amount by its percentage.

2. *What are the three main types of 'accountant's pricing'?*
   Cost plus, contribution and bottom-up (Hubbart).

3. *What's the difference between price elasticity and price sensitivity?*
   Elasticity is how much demand there is, sensitivity is how much you can vary the price for a given market.

4. *How do you find contribution – and what is it?*
   It's sales less variable costs – it's what you have left once you take the direct costs from the SP.

5. *What's the formula to calculate the BEP if you want to find the sales in money (not units)?*
   Divide the total fixed costs by the CM%.

Chapter 6

1. *What's a forecast?*
   It's a short-term prediction of levels of trade that lets you plan ahead. You start by forecasting volumes then look at purchasing, staffing and any other relevant areas.

2.. *Who does it?*
   Departmental managers who know what's happening in their areas.

3. *What's a budget?*
   It's a formal plan for the business for the year ahead. It's not just financial but also looks at marketing and staffing.

4. *What's a cash forecast?*
   It's a plan that shows when cash will be coming into, and going out of, the bank account. You could also use one for your own finances.

5. *Is a deficit on the month a problem?*
   It's the cumulative, carried forward figure that's important. Ideally that should be a positive figure but if not you may be able to borrow money on a short-term basis to cover a temporary shortfall.

6. *Why bother with the Outstanding column?*
   You normally need to do a balance sheet so if you work out the figures when doing the cash budget it's far easier to assemble the BS later.

Chapter 7

1. *What is liquidity?*
    It's how much money you have to run the business. The working capital (current assets less current liabilities) can be used to give a current ratio – but stock takes time to convert to cash and so a more useful ratio is the liquidity or the acid test – the proportion of debtors and cash to current liabilities.

2. *How much do you order?*
    You order what you need to run the business. By accurate forecasting and the use of par stocks you can keep sufficient stocks to satisfy customer needs while not tying up too much cash or space in stocks.

3. *How do you measure stock levels?*
    By calculating stock days and by the total value. Par levels help keep the levels stable.

4. *What's the best place to keep cash?*
    In the bank. If it has to be in the business then in a safe or secure place.

5. *What's the best way to store goods?*
    In accordance with health and safety regulations and in a tidy and organized format.

6. *How do you manage debtors?*
    By ensuring that invoices are correct when mailed and that collection calls are made on a timely basis. Good credit control is reliant on all areas of the business working together.

Chapter 8

1. *What do 'standard quantity' and 'standard price' mean?*
    Standard means budget – so it's the volume and the price that you have budgeted to achieve. They are sometimes abbreviated to read STDQ and STDP.

2. *Why is a standard recipe important for airline catering?*
    Airline catering is a very high volume, tight margin sector. What may seem minimal changes to recipes can have a high financial impact and hence standards have to be very strictly maintained to achieve profits. Standard costing is very important in this sector.

3. *How can standard costing be used in a rooms department's sales variance analysis?*
    Where actual revenues vary from budget you can also identify how much is

due to changes in achieved average room rate, and how much to changes in occupancy.

4. *How can standard costing help to predict payroll costs?*

You usually use standard costing to look back at what actually happened but you could also ask What If? and use the technique to predict the financial impact of proposed changes to hours and pay rates.

5. *What are the two approaches to standard costing?*

One finds the variance and then the cost of these. The other looks at the total costs (or revenues) and then finds the difference.

Chapter 9

1. *The Number One Rule with all work is...*

Save the file frequently. **Do backups** of all your work every time you update it.

And please – if you use a home-based machine (or somebody else's) please make sure you have a sophisticated virus-checker installed!

8. *Why is spreadsheet design important?*

You may want to use this spreadsheet again. If you design it well then you can use it easily and accurately again and again with the minimum of effort. Also, you want it to be effective in terms of appearance for the end-user, so that they understand what you want to 'say'. Good design can communicate figures very effectively and persuade others to your point of view.

9. *Why should I bother learning about charts?*

You can use them to present information more effectively- a picture's worth a thousand words! Break even charts can also help in making decisions.

Chapter 10

1. *How many people are involved in a partnership?*

Two or more – and normally up to 20. One person on their own is called a sole trader. Partners may be unequal – that is, they do not all have to invest equal amounts of money or skills.

2. *What's your financial liability if you are a sole trader?*

Everything! You are fully, solely, responsible for the debts of the business.

3. *What does 'return on equity' mean?*

Equity means shareholders' funds and comprises shares, share premium, retained earnings and profits. The return is the profit expressed as a percentage of this equity.

4. *Is the chairman's statement relevant to the annual report?*
    Yes, but needs to be read in conjunction with the rest of the report. They tend to emphasise the good things that have happened during the year and smooth over the less good.

5. *If a hotel group owns and operates a business is this likely to be a franchise or a management contract?*
    A franchise. If it were a management contract then typically a property company would own the actual building but would not be interested in running it – just collecting the profits.

Index